# How to Train a Wild Elephant

## And Other Adventures in Mindfulness

Jan Chozen Bays, MD

SHAMBHALA
BOSTON & LONDON || 2011

Shambhala Publications, Inc.
Horticultural Hall
300 Massachusetts Avenue
Boston, Massachusetts 02115
www.shambhala.com

14 13 12 11 10 9 8 7 6

Printed in the United States of America

♾This edition is printed on acid-free paper that meets the American National Standards Institute z39.48 Standard.
♻This book is printed on 30% postconsumer recycled paper. For more information please visit www.shambhala.com.

Distributed in the United States by Random House, Inc., and in Canada by Random House of Canada Ltd

Library of Congress Cataloging-in-Publication Data
Bays, Jan Chozen.
How to train a wild elephant: and other adventures in mindfulness/Jan Chozen Bays.—1st ed.
p. cm.
ISBN 978-1-59030-817-2 (pbk.: alk. paper)
1. Spiritual life—Buddhism. 2. Consciousness—Religious aspects—Buddhism. 3. Attention—Religious aspects—Buddhism. 4. Awareness—Religious aspects—Buddhism. I. Title. II. Title: And other adventures in mindfulness.
BQ5670.B39 2011
294.3'4435—dc22
2011006476

# Contents

# HOW TO TRAIN A WILD ELEPHANT

# Introduction

People often say to me, "I'd love to practice mindfulness, but I'm so busy I can't seem to find the time."

Most people think of mindfulness as something they must squeeze into an already full schedule of working, raising children, caring for a home. In truth, making mindfulness part of your life is more like a game of connect the dots, or like a paint-by-numbers kit. Do you remember those pictures where each small area is labeled with a number that tells you which color to use? As you filled in all the brown areas, then the greens and the blues, a pleasing picture begins to emerge.

Mindfulness practice is like that. You begin with one small area of your life, let's say how you answer the phone. Each time the phone rings, you pause to take three long, slow breaths before you pick it up. You do this for a week or so, until it becomes a habit. Then you add another mindfulness practice, such as mindful eating. Once this way of being present is integrated into your life, you add another. Gradually you are present and aware for more and more moments of the day. The pleasing experience of an awakened life begins to emerge.

The exercises in this book point to many different spaces in your life that you can begin to fill in with the warm colors of open-hearted mindfulness. I am a meditation teacher, and I live at a Zen monastery in Oregon. I'm also a pediatrician, a wife, a mother, and a grandmother, so I understand well how stressful and challenging daily life can become. I developed many of these exercises to help me be more aware, happy, and at ease within the flow of a busy life. I offer this collection to anyone who would like to become more fully present and enjoy the small moments of their life. You don't have to go to a monthlong meditation retreat or move to a monastery to restore peace and balance to your life. They are already available to you. Bit by bit, daily mindfulness practice will help you uncover satisfaction and fulfillment in the very life you are living now.

### WHAT IS MINDFULNESS AND WHY IS IT IMPORTANT?

In recent years, interest in mindfulness has grown enormously among researchers, psychologists, physicians, educators, and among the general public. There's now a significant body of scientific research indicating the benefits of mindfulness for mental and physical health. But what exactly do we mean by "mindfulness"?

Here's the definition I like to use:

> Mindfulness is deliberately paying full attention to what is happening around you and within you—in your body, heart, and mind. Mindfulness is awareness without criticism or judgment.

Sometimes we are mindful, and sometimes we are not. A good example is paying attention to your hands on the steering wheel of a car. Remember when you were first learning to drive, and how the car wobbled and wove its way along the road as your hands clumsily jerked the wheel back and forth, correcting and overcorrecting? You were wide awake, completely focused on the mechanics of driving. After a while your hands learned to steer well, making subtle and automatic adjustments. You could keep the car moving smoothly ahead without paying any conscious attention to your hands. You could drive, talk, eat, and listen to the radio, all at the same time.

Thus arises the experience we have all had, of driving on automatic pilot. You open the car door, search for your keys, back carefully out of the driveway, and . . . you pull into the parking garage at work. Wait a minute! What happened to twenty miles and forty minutes between house and job? Were the lights red or green? Your mind took a vacation, in some pleasant or distressing realm, as your body deftly maneuvered your car through flowing traffic and stoplights, suddenly awakening as you arrived at your destination.

Is that bad? It's not bad in the sense of something you should feel ashamed or guilty about. If you are able to drive to work on autopilot for years without having an accident, that's pretty skillful! We could say that it's sad, though, because when we spend a lot of time with our body doing one thing while our mind is on vacation somewhere else, it means that we aren't really present for much of our life. When we aren't present, it makes us feel vaguely but persistently dissatisfied. This sense of dissatisfaction, of a gap between us and everything and everyone else, is the essential problem of human life. It leads to those moments when we are pierced with a feeling of deep doubt and loneliness.

The Buddha called it the First Truth: the fact that every person will at some time experience this kind of distress. There are many happy moments in our lives, of course, but when our friends go home, when we are lonely or tired, when we feel disappointed or sad or betrayed, then dissatisfaction and unhappiness emerge once again.

We all try over-the-counter remedies—food, drugs, sex, overwork, alcohol, movies, shopping, gambling—to relieve the pain of ordinary life as a human being. All of these remedies work for a little while, but most of them have side effects—such as being in debt, blacking out, getting arrested, or losing someone we love—so they only increase our distress in the long run.

The labels on over-the-counter remedies say, "For temporary relief of symptoms only. If symptoms persist, see your doctor." Over the course of many years I have found one reliable remedy for the relief of recurrent discomfort and unhappiness. I have prescribed it for myself and for many other people, with excellent results. It is regular mindfulness practice.

Much of our dissatisfaction with life will disappear, and many simple joys will emerge, if we can learn to be present with things just as they are.

You've already experienced moments of mindful awareness. Everyone can recall at least one time when they were completely awake, when everything became clear and vivid. We call these peak moments. They can happen when we experience something unusually beautiful or poignant, such as the birth of a child or the passing of a loved one. It can also happen when our car goes into a skid. Time slows down as we watch the accident unfold or not. But it doesn't have to be dramatic.

It can happen on an ordinary walk, as we turn a corner and everything is, for a moment, luminous.

What we call peak moments are times when we are completely aware. Our life and our awareness are undivided, at one. At these times the gap between us and everything else closes and suffering disappears. We feel satisfied. Actually we are beyond satisfaction and dissatisfaction. We are present. We are Presence. We get a tantalizing taste of what Buddhists call the enlightened life.

These moments inevitably fade, and there we are again, separate and grumpy about it. We can't force peak moments or enlightenment to happen. The tools of mindfulness, however, can help us close the gaps that cause our unhappiness. Mindfulness unifies our body, heart, and mind, bringing them together in focused attention. When we are thus unified, the barrier between "me" and "everything else" becomes thinner and thinner until, in a moment, it vanishes! For a while, often a brief moment or occasionally a lifetime, all is whole, all is holy, and at peace.

## THE BENEFITS OF MINDFULNESS

There are many benefits of mindfulness practice. Research on happiness conducted by Brown and Ryan at the University of Rochester shows "people high in mindfulness are models of flourishing and positive mental health." It is good for all ailments your heart and mind, and even of your body. But don't believe me just because I said so. Try the exercises in this book for a year and discover how they change your own life.

Here are a few of the benefits of mindfulness that I have found.

## 1. Mindfulness Conserves Energy

It is fortunate that we can learn to do tasks skillfully. It is unfortunate that this skill enables us to go unconscious as we do them. It is unfortunate because when we go unconscious, we are missing out on large parts of our life. When we "check out," our mind tends to go to one of three places: the past, the future, or the fantasy realm. These three places have no reality outside our imagination. Right here where we are is the only place, and right now is the only time where we are actually alive.

The capacity of the human mind to recall the past is a unique gift. It helps us learn from our errors and change an unhealthy life direction. However, when the mind doubles back to the past, it often begins to ruminate endlessly on our past mistakes. "If only I'd said this . . . , then she would have said that . . . ." Unfortunately the mind seems to think we are very stupid. It calls up the errors of our past over and over, blaming and criticizing us repeatedly. We wouldn't pay to rent and watch the same painful movie two hundred fifty times, but somehow we let our mind replay a bad memory over and over, each time experiencing the same distress and shame. We wouldn't remind a child two hundred fifty times of a small mistake he or she made, but somehow we allow our mind to continue to call up the past and to inflict anger and shame upon our own inner small being. It seems that our mind is afraid that we will fall prey to bad judgment, ignorance, or inattention yet again. It doesn't believe that actually we are smart—smart enough to learn from one mistake, and not to repeat it.

Ironically, a mind filled with anxiety is likely to create what it most fears. The anxious mind doesn't realize that when it pulls us into daydreams of regret about the past, we are not attending to the present. When we are unable to be present, we tend not to act wisely or skillfully. We are more likely to do the very thing the mind worries we will do.

The capacity of the human mind to plan for the future is another of our unique gifts. It gives us a road map and compass to steer by. It decreases the chances that we will make a wrong turn and end up caught in a long detour. It increases the chances that we will arrive at the end of life satisfied with our life path and what we have accomplished.

Unfortunately the mind, in its anxiety for us, tries to make plans for a huge number of possible futures, most of which will never arrive. This constant leapfrogging into the future is a waste of our mental and emotional energy. The most important way we can prepare for the unknown-to-come is to make a reasonable plan and then to pay attention to what is happening right now. Then we can greet what flows toward us with a clear, flexible mind and an open heart, ready and able to modify our plan according to the reality of the moment.

The mind also enjoys excursions into realms of fantasy, where it creates an internal video of a new and different me, famous, handsome, powerful, talented, successful, wealthy, and loved. The capacity of the human mind to fantasize is wonderful, the basis of all our creativity. It allows us to imagine new inventions, create new art and music, arrive at new scientific hypotheses, and to make plans for everything from new buildings to new chapters of our lives. Unfortunately, it can become an escape, an escape from whatever is uncomfortable about the present moment, an escape from the anxiety of not knowing what is actually moving toward us, an escape from the fear that the next moment (or hour or day or year) could bring us difficulties or even death. Incessant fantasizing and daydreaming are different from directed creativity. Creativity comes from resting the mind in neutral, allowing it to clear itself and provide a fresh canvas on which new ideas, equations, poems, melodies, or colorful strokes can appear.

When we allow the mind to rest in the present, full of what is actually happening right now, redirecting it away from repeated fruitless, energy-sapping excursions into the past, future, or fantasy realms, we are doing something very important. We are conserving the energy of the mind. It remains fresh and open, ready to respond to whatever appears before it.

This may sound trivial, but it is not. Ordinarily our mind does not rest. Even at night it is active, generating dreams from a mix of anxieties and the events of our life. We know that our body cannot function well without rest, so we give it at least a few hours to lie down and relax each night. We forget, though, that our mind needs rest, too. Where it finds rest is in the present moment, where it can lie down and relax into the flow of events.

Mindfulness practice reminds us not to fritter our mental energy away in trips to past and future, but to keep returning to this very place, to rest in what is happening in this very time.

### 2. MINDFULNESS TRAINS AND STRENGTHENS THE MIND

We are all aware that the human body can be trained. We can become more flexible (gymnasts and acrobats), more graceful (ballet dancers), more skilled (piano players), and stronger (weight lifters). We are less aware that there are many aspects of mind that can be cultivated. Just before his enlightenment the Buddha described the qualities of mind and heart that he had developed over many years. He observed that his mind had become "concentrated, purified, bright, unblemished, malleable, wieldy, rid of imperfections, imperturbable." When we practice mindfulness, we learn to lift the mind up out of its habitual preoccupations and place it down in a place of our choosing in order to illuminate some aspect of our life. We are training the mind to be light, powerful, and flexible but also able to concentrate on what we ask it to focus on.

The Buddha spoke of taming the mind. He said it was like taming a wild forest elephant. Just as an untamed elephant can do damage, trampling crops and injuring people, so the untamed, capricious mind can cause harm to us and those around us. Our human minds have a much larger capacity and power than we realize. Mindfulness is a potent tool for training the mind, allowing us to access and use the mind's true potential for insight, kindness, and creativity.

The Buddha pointed out that when a wild elephant is first captured and led out of the jungle, it has to be tethered to a stake. In the case of our mind, that stake takes the form of whatever we attend to in our mindfulness practice—for example, the breath, a mouthful of food, or our posture. We anchor the mind by returning it over and over to one thing. This calms the mind and rids it of distractions.

A wild elephant has many wild habits. It runs away when humans approach. It attacks when frightened. Our mind is similar. When it senses danger, it runs away from the present. It might run to pleasant fantasies, to thoughts of future revenge, or just go numb. If it is frightened, it may attack other people in an angry outburst, or it may attack inwardly, in silent but corrosive self-criticism.

In the time of the Buddha, elephants were trained to go into battle, to obey commands without fleeing from the din and chaos of war. Similarly, a mind trained through mindfulness can stand steady under the rapidly changing conditions of modern life. Once our mind is tamed, we can remain calm and stable as we encounter the inevitable difficulties the world brings us. Eventually we don't run from problems but see them as a way to test and strengthen our physical and mental stability.

Mindfulness helps us become aware of the mind's habitual and conditioned patterns of escape and allows us to try an alternative way of being in the world. That alternative is resting our awareness in the actual events of the present moment, the sounds heard by the ear, the sensations felt by the skin, the colors and shapes taken in by the eyes. Mindfulness helps stabilize the heart and mind so they are not so badly tossed around by the unexpected things that arrive in our life. If we practice mindfulness patiently and long enough, eventually we become interested in everything that happens, curious about what we can learn even from adversity and, eventually, even from our own death.

### 3. MINDFULNESS IS GOOD FOR THE ENVIRONMENT

Most of this mental activity, circling around endlessly in the realms of the past, future, and fantasy life, is not only pointless, it is destructive. How? It is fueled by an ecologically harmful fuel. That fuel is anxiety.

You might wonder, how is anxiety related to ecology? When we talk of ecology, we usually think of a world of physical relationships among living beings, such as the relationships among the bacteria, fungi, plants, and animals in a forest. But ecological relationships are based upon energy exchange, and anxiety is an energy.

We might be aware that if a mother is chronically anxious,

it could affect her unborn child adversely, through changes in blood flow and in the nutrients and hormones that bathe the baby. In the same way when we are anxious, it affects the multitude of living "beings" inside of us—our heart, our liver, our gut, the billions of bacteria in our gut, our skin. The negative effects of our fear and anxiety are not confined to the container of our body. Our anxiety also affects every being we come in contact with. Fear is a highly contagious state of mind, one that spreads quickly through families, communities, and whole nations.

Mindfulness involves resting our mind in a place where there is no anxiety, no fear. In fact, in that place we find the opposite. We discover resourcefulness, courage, and a quiet happiness.

Where is that "place"? It is not a geographic location. It is not a location in time. It is the flowing time and place of the present moment. Anxiety is fueled by thoughts of past and future. When we drop those thoughts, we drop anxiety and find ourselves at ease. How do we drop thoughts? We drop thoughts by temporarily withdrawing energy from the thinking function of the mind and redirecting it to the awareness function of the mind. This deliberate infusion of awareness is the essence of mindfulness. Relaxed, alert awareness is the antidote to anxiety and fear, both our own and others'. It is an ecologically beneficial way to live a human life; it changes the atmosphere for the better.

4. MINDFULNESS CREATES INTIMACY

Our essential hunger is not for food but for intimacy. When intimacy is missing in our lives, we feel isolated from other beings, alone, vulnerable, and unloved in the world.

We habitually look to other people to fulfill our needs for

intimacy. However, our partners and friends cannot always be there for us in the way we need. Luckily a profound experience of intimacy is always accessible to us—all it requires is that we turn around and move toward life. This will require courage. We have to intentionally open our senses, becoming deliberately aware of what is going on both inside our body and heart/mind, and also outside, in our environment.

Mindfulness is a deceptively simple tool for helping us to be aware. It is a practice that helps us wake up, be present, and live life more abundantly. It helps fill in the gaps in our day, the many times we go unconscious and are not present for big chunks of our life. It is also a practice that will help us close the frustrating gap, the invisible shield that seems to exist between ourselves and other people.

### 5. MINDFULNESS STOPS OUR STRUGGLING AND CONQUERS FEAR

Mindfulness helps us stay present with experiences that aren't pleasant. Our usual tendency is to try to arrange the world and other people so that we are comfortable. We spend a lot of energy trying to make the temperature around us just right, the lighting just right, the fragrance in the air just right, the food just right, our beds and chairs just the right softness, the colors of our walls just right, the grounds around our homes just right, and the people around us—our children, intimate partners, friends, coworkers, and even pets—just right.

But, try as we might, things don't stay the way we want them. Sooner or later, our child throws a tantrum, dinner burns, the heating system breaks down, we become ill. If we are able to stay present and open, even to welcome experiences and people that aren't comfortable for us, they will lose their power to frighten us and make us react or flee. If we can do this over and over again, we will have gained an amazing power, rare in the human world—to be happy despite constantly changing conditions.

### 6. MINDFULNESS SUPPORTS OUR SPIRITUAL LIFE

Mindfulness tools are an invitation to bring attention to the many small activities of life. They are particularly helpful to people who would like to nurture a spiritual life in the midst of all the distractions of modern living. Zen master Suzuki Roshi said, "Zen is not some kind of excitement, but concentration on our usual everyday routine." Mindfulness practice brings our awareness back to this body, this time, this place. This is exactly where we can be touched by the eternal presence we call the Divine. When we are mindful, we are appreciating each moment of the particular life we have been given. Mindfulness is a way of expressing our gratitude for a gift that we can never repay. Mindfulness can become a constant prayer of gratitude.

Christian mystics speak of a "life of continuous prayer." What could this mean? How could it be possible when we are swept along in the speedy traffic of modern life, cutting corners continuously, without enough time to talk to our own family, let alone God?

True prayer is not petitioning, it is listening. Deep listening. When we listen deeply, we find that even the "sound" of our own thoughts is disruptive, even annoying. Letting go of thoughts, we enter a more profound inner stillness and receptivity. If this open silence can be held at our core, *as* our core, then we are no longer confused by trying to sort out and choose among our myriad competing inner voices. Our attention is no longer caught up in the emotional tangle within. It is directed outward. We are looking for the Divine in all appearances, listening to the Divine in all sounds, brushed by the Divine in all touches. As things move toward us, we respond appropriately, and then return to resting in inner silence. This is a life lived in faith, faith in the One Mind, a life of continuous prayer.

When we infuse one routine activity with mindfulness, then another and another, we are waking up to the mystery of each moment, unknowable until it arrives. As things come forward, we are ready to receive and respond. We are receptive to what is being given to us, moment by moment, by the Great Presence. They are simple gifts, warmth spreading through our hands as we hold a cup of tea, thousands of tiny caresses as clothing touches our skin, the complex music of raindrops, one more breath. When we are able to give full attention to the living truth of each moment, we enter the gate to a life of continuous prayer.

## MISUNDERSTANDINGS ABOUT MINDFULNESS

Although mindfulness is highly touted, people may easily misunderstand it. First, they may mistakenly believe that to practice mindfulness means to think hard about something. In mindfulness we use the thinking power of the mind only to initiate the practice ("Be aware of your posture today") and to remind us to return to the practice when the mind inevitably wanders during the day ("Return your awareness to your posture"). However, once we follow the mind's instructions and begin to use the method, we can let go of thoughts. When the thinking mind quiets down, it shifts into open awareness. Then we are anchored in the body, alert and present.

The second misunderstanding about mindfulness is that it

means doing everything *very slowly*. The speed at which we do things is not the point. It is possible to perform a task slowly and still be inattentive. Actually, when we move faster, we often need to become more attentive if we want to avoid errors. To use some of the mindfulness tools in this book, you may need to slow down—for example, while practicing mindful eating. For other exercises you will be asked to slow down briefly, to bring the mind and body together before reengaging with your regular activities—for example, resting the mind for three breaths. Other tasks can be done at any speed, such as the exercise that involves paying attention to the bottoms of the feet while sitting, walking, or running.

A third common misunderstanding is to think of mindfulness as a program of time-limited exercises, such as a thirty-minute period of sitting meditation. Mindfulness is helpful to the extent that it spreads out into all the activities of our life, bringing the light of heightened awareness, curiosity, and a sense of discovery to the mundane activities of life, getting up in the morning, brushing teeth, walking through a door, answering a phone, listening to someone talk.

HOW TO USE THIS BOOK

This book offers a wide variety of ways to bring mindfulness into your daily life. We call them "mindfulness exercises." You could also think of them as mindfulness "seeds," seeds to plant and grow mindfulness in the many nooks and corners of your life, seeds you can watch as they grow and bear fruit each day.

Each exercise has several sections. First there is a description of the task and some ideas about how to remind yourself to do it throughout the day and week. Next is a section entitled

"Discoveries," which includes people's observations, insights, or difficulties with the task, along with any relevant research findings. In the section called "Deeper Lessons" I explore the themes and larger life lessons connected with the exercise. Each exercise is like a window, giving us a glimpse of what an awakened life would be like. Lastly there are a few "Final Words," which sum up the exercise or inspire you to continue letting it unfold.

One way to use the book is to start each week by reading only the description of the task and how to remind yourself to do it. No peeking ahead! Post your reminder words or pictures where you'll see them during the day in order to remember the task. Midweek you could read the Discoveries section for that particular exercise to see what experiences and insights other people have had in trying it. This might change how you approach the exercise. At the end of the week you could read the Deeper Lessons section before moving on to a new exercise.

You might want to do what we do at the monastery: we begin with the first mindfulness exercise and move through the year in order, practicing each one for one week. You could start a new task each Monday and finish reading or journaling about a task on the following Sunday. You can also skip around if a specific exercise or theme seems suited to the conditions of your life this week. Sometimes we continue trying the same mindfulness practice for two or three weeks if it continues to yield insights or we'd like to get better at doing it.

It's fun to do these practices with other people, as we do at the monastery. You might form a mindfulness practice group that picks an exercise to use for a week or two and then meets so that people can share what they've learned. There's a lot of laughter at our weekly discussions. It's important to take our "failures" lightly. Each person has different experiences, insights, and funny stories to tell about his or her attempts—and failures—to do these exercises.

We began the practice of taking on a new mindfulness tool or task each week at the monastery about twenty years ago. The idea came from a man who had lived in a community that followed the teachings of the mystic Gurdjieff. He explained that it didn't matter if you succeeded with the task or not. Sometimes *not doing* the exercise could teach you more than doing it, because you got to look at why you didn't do it. What was behind it—laziness, old aversions, or just spacing out? The point is to live more and more in a conscious way. Gurdjieff called this "self-remembering." In Buddhism we call it awakening to our true self. It is waking up to our life as it actually is, not the fantasy we often live out in our mind.

### Reminders

Over the years, we have found that the most difficult part of our weekly mindfulness practices is just remembering to do them. So we've invented various ways to remind ourselves throughout the day and week. Often we stick words or small images up around the monastery where we are likely to encounter them. You can print out our simple reminders at www.shambhala.com/howtotrain. I've described these in the book, but please be creative and invent your own.

### A Mindfulness Practice Notebook

To help you get the most out of these practices, I recommend using a notebook to record what you experience and learn as you work with each mindfulness exercise. If you're working through the book with a group, you can bring the notebook to your discussion sessions to remind you about the discoveries you made and the obstacles you encountered. Having a notebook on your desk or bedside table also helps as a reminder to do the practice of the week.

### CONTINUING ON

We hope that once we use a mindfulness tool for a week, it will stick with us and become part of our ever-expanding capacity for mindfulness. Being human, however, we often lapse back into old behaviors and unconscious habit patterns. That is why at the monastery we have continued to use these mindfulness practices for two decades, and to invent new ones. This is one of the most wonderful aspects of the path of mindfulness and awakening. It has no end!

# 1

# Use Your Nondominant Hand

---

The Exercise: Use your nondominant hand for some ordinary tasks each day. These could include brushing your teeth, combing your hair, or eating with the non-dominant hand for at least part of each meal. If you're up for a big challenge, try using the nondominant hand when writing or when eating with chopsticks.

---

REMINDING YOURSELF

One way to remember this task throughout your day is to put a Band-Aid on your dominant hand. When you notice it, switch hands and use the nondominant hand. You could also tape a small sign on your bathroom mirror that says "Left Hand" (if you're right-handed). Or tape a paper cutout of a hand to your mirror, refrigerator, or your desk—wherever you're likely to see it.

Another approach is to tape something to the handle of your toothbrush, reminding you to brush your teeth with the nondominant hand.

## DISCOVERIES

This experiment always evokes laughter. We discover that the nondominant hand is quite clumsy. Using it brings us back to what Zen teachers call "beginner's mind." Our dominant hand might be forty years old, but the nondominant hand is much younger, perhaps about two or three years old. We have to learn all over again how to hold a fork and how to get it into our mouths without stabbing ourselves. We might begin to brush our teeth very awkwardly with the nondominant hand, and when we aren't looking our dominant hand will reach out and take the toothbrush or fork away! It is just like a bossy older sister who says, "Hey, you little klutz, let me do it for you!"

Struggling to use the nondominant hand can awaken our compassion for anyone who is clumsy or unskilled, such as a person who has had disabilities, injuries, or a stroke. We briefly see how much we take for granted scores of simple movements that many people cannot make. Using chopsticks with the nondominant hand is a humbling experience. If you want to eat a meal in under an hour and not end up spilling food all over, you have to be very attentive.

## DEEPER LESSONS

This task illustrates how strong and unconscious our habits are and how difficult they are to change without awareness and determination. This task helps us bring beginner's mind to any activity—such as eating—that we do several times a day, often with only partial awareness.

Using the nondominant hand reveals our impatience. It can help us become more flexible and discover that we are never too old to learn new tricks. If we practice using the nondominant hand frequently, over time we can watch our skill develop. I have been practicing using my left hand for several years and I now forget which hand is the "right" hand to use. This could have practical benefits. If I lose the use of my dominant hand, as a number of my relatives did after strokes, I won't be "left" helpless. When we develop a new skill, we realize that there are many other abilities lying dormant within us. This insight can arouse confidence that, with practice, we can transform ourselves in many ways, moving toward more flexibility and freedom in life. If we are willing to make the effort, over time, we can awaken the skills arising from the natural wisdom within us and let them function in our daily life.

Zen master Suzuki Roshi said, "In the beginner's mind there are many possibilities, but in the expert's there are few." Mindfulness enables us to keep returning to the unlimited possibilities that are always emerging from the great birthing place of the present moment.

---

Final Words: To bring possibilities into your life, unfold beginner's mind in all situations.

---

## 2

# Leave No Trace

---

**The Exercise:** Choose one room of your house and for one week try leaving no trace that you've used that space. The bathroom or kitchen works best for most people. If you've been doing something in that room, cooking a meal or taking a shower, clean up in such a way that you leave no signs that you've been there, except perhaps the odor of food or fragrance of soap.

---

REMINDING YOURSELF

Put a sign in the room you've chosen that says, "Leave No Trace."

In Zen paintings turtles symbolize this practice of leaving no traces, because they sweep the sand with their tails as they creep along, wiping out their footprints. Instead of a written sign, you could also use small pictures of turtles as reminders.

Often, we leave rooms a bit messier than when we entered. We think, "I'll clean it up later." Later never comes, until the mess is unbearable, and we become irritated enough to undertake a thorough cleaning. Or we get annoyed at someone else for not doing their part in the housework. How much easier if we take care of things right away. Then we don't have to feel growing annoyance at the gathering mess.

This task helps us become aware of the tendency to turn away from doing certain things, even small things that we could take care of during the day but somehow don't have the motivation to do. We could pick up the trash on the sidewalk as we walk by, or the paper towel that missed the bin in the washroom. We could straighten the pillows on the couch after we get up, or wash our coffee cup instead of putting it in the sink, and we could put tools away even though we'll be using them again tomorrow.

One person observed that becoming mindful about leaving no traces in one room spread out to include other areas. Washing her dirty dishes immediately after eating led to making her bed immediately after arising, and then to cleaning the little hairs out of the drain right after a shower. We have to summon the initial energy, but thereafter, energy seems to breed more energy.

## DEEPER LESSONS

This exercise puts a spotlight on our tendency to be lazy. The word *lazy* is a description, not a criticism. If we live less than wholeheartedly, we often leave messes for others to clean up. It is so easy to wash the dishes but not put them back in the cupboard. It is so easy to skip meditation or prayer when our life gets hectic.

This task also brings our awareness to the many small things that support our life and work all day long—the spoons and forks that feed us, the clothing that keeps us warm, the rooms that shelter us. When we wash, dry, sweep, fold, and put away our things with mindfulness, it becomes an expression of gratitude for their silent service.

Zen master Dogen wrote specific instructions for the cooks in his monastery. "Clean the chopsticks, ladles, and all other utensils; handle them with equal care and awareness, putting everything back where it naturally belongs." There is something satisfying about washing things that are dirty and putting things in order, and about treating everything that serves us with care, whether plastic plates or delicate china. Our mind seems "cleaner" and our life less complicated when we've cleaned up the space and things around us. A friend told me about hauling pounds of old clothing, long-expired medication, and trash out of an elderly aunt's house. He said, "At first she seemed worried, but then she relaxed, and with every bag we took out she seemed to get a year younger."

The sense of satisfaction from leaving no traces may be a reflection of our deep desire to leave the world at least no worse than when we entered it, and hopefully, to leave it a bit better. Ideally the only traces we will leave will be the ways we have loved, inspired, taught, or served others. This is what will have the most positive effect on people in the future.

---

Final Words: First practice leaving no traces. Then practice leaving things better than you found them.

---

# 3

# Filler Words

The Exercise: Become aware of the use of "filler" words and phrases and try to eliminate them from your speech. Fillers are words that do not add meaning to what you're saying, such as "um," "ah," "so," "well," "like," "you know," "kind of," and "sort of." Additional filler words enter our vocabulary from time to time. Recent additions might include "basically" and "anyway."

In addition to eliminating filler words, see if you can notice why you tend to use them—in what situations and for what purpose?

REMINDING YOURSELF

It is mortifyingly difficult to notice yourself using filler words at first. You will probably have to enlist the help of friends or family members. Children will love catching and correcting their parents using filler words. Ask them to raise their hands when they hear you use a filler word. At first, hands will pop up and down with annoying frequency, and so unconscious is this habit that you may have to ask them to tell you what filler word you just uttered!

Another way to be able to hear the filler words you use and their frequency is to record yourself talking. Ask a roommate, spouse, or child to use his or her cell phone or video camera to record you in conversation or while you're talking on the phone. Play it back and tabulate the fillers you use and their frequency.

## DISCOVERIES

At the monastery we have found this to be one of the most challenging mindfulness practices we do. It is frustratingly hard to hear your own filler words and catch them before they are spoken—unless you are a trained speaker. In the Toastmasters clubs (groups that train in public speaking) there are people assigned to tally filler words during talks, assisting members as they learn to be effective speakers. Once you begin to hear filler words, you will hear them everywhere, on the radio and TV and in everyday conversation. A typical teenager uses the filler word *like* an estimated two hundred thousand times a year! You will also notice which speakers do not use them, and become aware of how the absence of filler words makes a speech more effective and powerful. For example, listen to Martin Luther King, Jr., the Dalai Lama, or President Barack Obama's speeches with an ear for filler words.

Filler words seem to serve several functions. They are space holders, telling the listener that you are going to start speaking or that you are not finished speaking yet. "So . . . I told him what I thought of his idea and then, um, I said, like, you know . . ." Filler words also soften what we say, making it less definite or assertive. "So anyway, I, you know, think we should, basically, kind of go ahead with this project." Are we afraid of provoking a reaction or of being wrong? We wouldn't want a president or doctor who spoke in such a wishy-washy way. Filler words can become an obstruction to the listening audience when they so dilute the meaning as to render it silly. "Jesus sort of said, 'Love your, you know, neighbor, as, sort of, like, yourself.'"


### DEEPER LESSONS

Filler words have become common only in the last fifty years. Is this because there is less emphasis in schools on precise speech, elocution, and good debating skills? Or, in today's multicultural, postmodern world, where truth is often regarded as relative, have we purposely moved to speaking in less definitive ways? Are we afraid to say something that might be politically incorrect or provoke a reaction from our audience? Are we sinking into moral relativism? If this trend continues, we will find ourselves saying, "Stealing is like, sort of, in a way, wrong."

When our mind is clear, we can speak in a straightforward way, with precision, and without insulting others.

This mindfulness tool shows how entrenched unconscious behaviors are, and how difficult they are to change. Unconscious habits such as using filler words are just that, unconscious. As long as they remain unconscious, they are impossible to change. Only when we bring the light of awareness to a pattern of behavior do we begin to have some space to work to modify them. Even then, it is very difficult to change an ingrained behavior. As soon as we stop working actively to change an unwanted habit, it quickly returns. If we want to change ourselves, if we want to realize our potential, it takes kindness, determination, and steady, sustained practice.

---

**Final Words:** "I think you're all enlightened until you open your mouths."—Zen master Suzuki Roshi

---

# 4

# Appreciate Your Hands

The Exercise: Several times a day, when your hands are busy, watch them as though they belonged to a stranger. Also look at them when they are still.

REMINDING YOURSELF

Write the words "Watch Me" on the back of your hand.

If your work makes this impossible, put on a ring that you don't usually wear. (If you are not allowed to wear rings, say because you work in an operating room, you can use the time of hand washing or putting on surgical gloves to become aware of your hands as though they belonged to a stranger.)

If you don't usually wear nail polish, you could remind yourself to watch your hands by painting your nails for a week. Or, if you do wear polish, you could wear an unusual color.

## DISCOVERIES

Our hands are very skilled at all sorts of tasks, and they can do many of them by themselves, without much direction from our mind. It's fun to watch them at work, busily living their own life. Hands can do so much! The two hands can work together or do different things at the same time.

While doing this exercise we noticed that each person has characteristic hand gestures. Our hands wave about when we talk, almost by themselves. We noticed that our hands change over time. Look at your hands and imagine them as they were when you were a baby, then imagine them changing as you grew older, until they reach the present time and state. Then imagine them growing older, becoming lifeless when you die, then dissolving back into the earth.

Even when we are asleep our hands are caring for us, pulling up the blankets, holding the body next to us, turning off the alarm clock.

## DEEPER LESSONS

We are being taken care of all the time. Some Zen teachers say that the way the body takes care of us, without our even being aware of it, is an example of the beautiful and continuous functioning of our Original Nature, the inherent goodness and wisdom of our being. Our hand pulls back from fire before we even register heat, our eyes blink before we are aware of a sharp sound, our hand reaches out to catch something before we know it is falling. The right and left hands work together, each one doing its half of a task. Drying dishes, one hand holds the dish and the other the towel. Cutting with a knife, one holds the vegetable while the other chops. They cooperate to wash each other.

There is a koan (a Zen teaching story) about the bodhisattva of compassion, who is called Kanzeon in Japanese, Kuan Yin in Chinese. She is often depicted with a thousand eyes, to see every person in need of comfort, and one thousand hands, each holding a different implement to aid them. Sometimes there is even an eye in the palm of each hand. The story is this:

One day the Zen monk Ungan asked Zen master Dogo, "How does the Bodhisattva Kanzeon use all those many hands and eyes?"

Dogo answered, "It is like a man in the middle of the night reaching behind his head for his pillow."

One of my students is a luthier, and he had insight into this story. Working inside the body of a guitar on a spot he could not see, he realized that his hands have "eyes." They can "see" the surface they are touching, in detail, and work on it, even in the dark. His inner eye and his hand were working together beautifully, just as a sleeping man "sees" his pillow and his hands naturally reach out to pull it under his head. In Zen we say this shows the way our innate wisdom and compassion work together when our mind is not in the way.

When we see clearly into the unity of all existence, we see that all things are working together, like the hands and eyes. As our hands would not hurt our eyes, our natural nature is not to hurt ourselves or each other.

**Final Words:** The two hands work together effortlessly to accomplish many wonderful things and they never harm each other. Could this become true for any two human beings?

# 5

# When Eating Just Eat

**The Exercise:** This week, when you're eating or drinking, don't do anything else. Sit down and take the time to enjoy what you are taking in. Open all the senses as you eat or drink. Look at the colors, shapes, surface textures. Attend to the smells and flavors in your mouth. Listen to the sounds of eating and drinking.

## REMINDING YOURSELF

Post a note on the table where you eat meals that says, "Just Eat." Also post this note wherever you are likely to snack.

Also post notes on objects that tend to distract you while you eat. For example, on your computer or TV, post the word "Eating" with an X through it as a reminder not to eat while using it.

## DISCOVERIES

This is not an easy task for most people. If you're on the go, walking from one place to another and about to take a sip of tea or coffee, you're going to need to stop, find a place to sit down, and savor it. If you're working on the computer, you're going to have to take both hands off the keyboard and turn your eyes away from the screen in order to savor a sip of coffee.

Eating has become part of our modern habit of perpetually multitasking. When we do this exercise, we discover anew how many other things we do while eating. We eat while walking, driving, watching TV or movies, reading, working on the computer, playing video games, and listening to music.

Once we eliminate those obvious activities, we come to a more subtle aspect of inattention—talking while eating. Our parents may have scolded us for talking with our mouths full, but we still find ourselves eating and talking simultaneously. While doing this task we learn to alternate eating and talking. In other words, if you want to talk, stop eating. Don't do them at the same time.

It is so common to socialize while eating that you may discover that you feel awkward eating alone in a restaurant without reading or otherwise distracting yourself. You might imagine that people are thinking, "Poor thing, no friends." You pick up a book or open your computer to show you are being productive and wouldn't "waste time" by "just eating." One problem with eating and doing other things is that it becomes "waist time," that is, time for extra food to go down unnoticed and end up on your waist!

In Japan and parts of Europe it is very rude to walk and eat or drink at the same time. The only food you can eat in Japan while standing up or walking is an ice-cream cone, because it might melt. People will stare at the boorish foreigner who buys fast food and walks down the street munching. Even fast food is taken home, arranged attractively, and served at a table.

Meals are times to slow down and truly enjoy the food, drink, and company.

## DEEPER LESSONS

Why do we feel compelled to multitask, to not waste time by just eating? It seems that our self-worth is based upon how much we can produce in a day, or how many items we can cross off our long "to do" list. Eating and drinking are activities that don't earn us money, a spouse, or a Nobel Prize, so we begin to think they have no value. During mindful-eating workshops many people say, "Oh, I just eat to get it over with so I can get on with my work." What if the most important work we do each day is to be truly present, even for only thirty minutes? What if the most important gift we can give to the world is not any kind of product or present, but is, instead, our *presence*?

When we are not paying attention, it is as if the food did not exist. We can clean our plate and still feel dissatisfied. We will keep on eating, stopping only when we are over-full and uncomfortable. If we eat with mindful awareness, then the experience of eating even one bite becomes rich and varied. Then we can eat until we feel inner satisfaction rather than eating until we feel "stuffed."

The Zen monk Thich Nhat Hanh writes,

There are some people who eat an orange but don't really eat it. They eat their sorrow, fear, anger; their past and future. They are not really present, with body and mind united. You need some training just to enjoy [your food]. It has come from the whole cosmos just for our nourishment . . . this is a miracle.

**Final Words:** When eating, just eat. When drinking, just drink. Mindfulness is the very best seasoning, for your food and for your entire life. Enjoy each bite, enjoy each moment!

## 6

# True Compliments

The Exercise: Once a day, think of someone close to you—a family member, a friend, or a coworker—and give them a genuine compliment. The closer the person is to you, the better, such as a child or a parent. (It doesn't count to tell a stranger at the post office that you like their scarf.) The more specific the compliment, the better. "I appreciate the way you answer the phone so cheerfully."

Become aware also of any compliments other people give you. Investigate the purpose of compliments and the effect on you of being given a compliment.

REMINDING YOURSELF

Post the word "Praise" or "Compliment" in places where you'll see it throughout the day.

Some people report that they were resistant to this task at first, because they feared their compliments wouldn't be genuine. They soon discovered many things they could be grateful for, and they were able to do the exercise. Some people realized as they did this task that they have a habitual stance that is critical, only noticing and remarking on problems. Undertaking this practice helped highlight and reverse this state of mind.

Other people commented that when they gave compliments, they noticed that the person receiving the compliment often blocked it. "Oh, I don't think my cookies are so good this time." Being given a compliment creates vulnerability. Some people may have become wary of compliments in adolescence, when they couldn't be sure if a compliment was meant sincerely or was designed to make them the butt of a joke. Perhaps they also began to give compliments in a joking way or rebutting a compliment as if it were a joke in order to protect themselves from potential embarrassment. One person reported that his parents had to teach him how to receive compliments. They advised, "Simply say, 'Thank you.' That's all the other person needs."

Another man described how he had actively studied the art of giving compliments because he had never been given anything but negative feedback when he was growing up in an alcoholic home. He found that giving compliments "lightens things up and shifts the energy to positive." He also found that his children, spouse, and employees seem to thrive when given genuine compliments.

There are some cultural differences in how compliments are received. In studies in China and Japan, 95 percent of responses to compliments were designed to deny or deflect the praise. In Asia it is normal to dismiss or back away from compliments, because one might be seen to lack humility. A husband would not compliment his wife in front of others, lest it seem that he is bragging.

Nonviolent Communication, an approach to effective conflict resolution, teaches that a compliment such as "You're so [adjective] . . ." tends to be disconnecting. They recommend centering compliments around something that touched you, because this type of compliment promotes a sense of connection and intimacy. "I was touched by how you took the time to bake fresh cookies for this meeting. Thank you."

This mindfulness exercise helps us become aware of the function and frequency of compliments in our relationships with others. Some compliments seem genuine while others seem aimed at getting something in return. When we first meet someone, or when we are courting, more compliments are exchanged. Later we seem to take those close to us for granted and stop expressing praise, gratitude, or appreciation.

## DEEPER LESSONS

Zen master Dogen wrote, "You should know that kind speech arises from kind mind, and kind mind from the seed of compassionate mind. You should ponder the fact that kind speech is not just praising the merit of others; it has the power to turn the destiny of the nation."

The Buddhist teachings describe three feeling tones we experience in reaction to people, objects, or events: positive (a happy feeling), negative (an irritated feeling), and neutral (no positive or negative feelings). When we feel positively about a person, we are more likely to beam a positive feeling tone toward them and to give them compliments. For example, we're naturally inclined to compliment someone we are courting or a cute baby who hasn't yet transformed into an obstinate toddler.

When someone becomes part of the furniture of our life, we forget to notice what they do and it doesn't occur to us to give them compliments. In fact, we may only comment on the negative, the things we see that we think need to be changed. Without our intending it, this can gradually impart a negative feeling tone to the entire relationship. The practice of actively noticing what a person does well and giving genuine compliments can add new warmth, intimacy, and responsiveness to a relationship.

Personal compliments about temporary or conditional qualities such as beauty make us a little uncomfortable. Why is this? Because we intuitively know that some qualities, such as physical beauty, are serendipitous intersections of genes and current cultural norms. We did not sculpt our handsome face. It is a temporary gift. We know that with time it will change into something with a double chin and many wrinkles. In even a year's time it could become defined as "ugly." Straight hair becomes popular for a few years, and girls with curly hair spend hours straightening it. Then curly hair comes into fashion. Most of the things we get compliments for are temporary—a slim figure, athletic ability, even intelligence. They are seldom qualities that we actually earned. This is why the best compliments are founded upon appreciation for how a person made you feel.

Below the temporary qualities that garner compliments lies our True Nature. In Buddhism this is called our Buddha nature;

in other religions it is called our divine nature. It is our essence. It is not based upon feelings, physical characteristics, or any kind of comparison. It cannot be inflated by compliments or diminished by criticism. There is nothing that you do can add to it, nothing you do can subtract from it. No matter what you have done wrong or right, no matter what has been done to you, it remains untouched. It does not increase when you are born or decrease when you die. It is the Eternal expressing itself as you.

---

**Final Words:** Kind words are a gift. They create wealth in the heart.

---

# 7

# Mindfulness of Posture

---

The Exercise: Several times a day, become aware of your posture. This has two aspects. First it means to become aware of what posture you are in and how it feels within the body. If you closed your eyes, what would be the clues that you are standing or sitting or lying down? For example, if you are sitting in a chair with your eyes closed, what tells you that you are in a body that is sitting? Where do you feel pressure or movement?

Being aware of posture also means to notice and adjust your posture many times a day. If you are slouching, gently straighten up.

A very good time to work with mindfulness of posture is at meals. Sit on the front edge of the chair with your feet planted on the floor, knees a bit apart. Straighten the spine to maximize room for breathing.

Other interesting times to become aware of posture include while standing in line, driving, lying down in bed, in meetings or classes, and while walking.

---

### REMINDING YOURSELF

Ask for help from your family or friends. Tell them you want reminders if your posture is slumped. Also look at your posture in mirrors and reflective windows. As you go by, stand so you can see your posture from the side. Does it need adjusting?

Place a little piece of colored tape or a small note that says "Posture" on the chair or on the table you use for meals.


### DISCOVERIES

People are often surprised to discover that they have poor posture. Their posture looks OK from the front, but when they see their reflections from the side, they are shocked to discover that their shoulders are slumped. We adjust our posture to different situations. At a job interview or an interesting lecture, we sit up straight; watching TV, we slump on the couch. It is easy to pick out those people who have had certain kinds of training, such as military officers, dancers, or royalty. They have a noticeably upright posture. Why is posture important for these people? There is a Spanish saying, "You can tell a priest even in a bathing suit," meaning that a religious person is distinguishable just by his or her outward demeanor, because this reflects an internal posture or alignment.

In Zen practice we put a lot of emphasis on posture, not only in the meditation hall but also sitting at the table, and even walking about. We walk with the hands held folded together at the waist, maintaining what Catholic nuns call "custody of the hands." When we pass each other in the walkways, we stop, put palms together, and bow. When we are given our work assignment for the day, we bow, grateful for a body that can work.

Four times a day during chanting services we do full prostrations down to the floor, where we take a posture of humility, head to the ground, putting down our self-obsessed minds and guarded hearts, lifting our palms from the floor to signify we are seeking to raise up our full potential for wisdom and compassion. Some days we do over a hundred of these full bows. People who are doing atonement practice for past wrongdoing may do 108 extra full prostrations each day. One Zen master did so many full bows each day that he developed a callus on his forehead. He said that he was an obstinate, stubborn fellow and needed to practice humility.

Japanese people bow many, many times each day. Often old people there are bent over and cannot straighten up. They do not mind this, saying that it helps them to keep on bowing to life and to be grateful for whatever it brings them.

### DEEPER LESSONS

Buddhist monk and teacher Ajahn Chah said, "Wisdom comes from being mindful in all postures. Your practice should begin as you awaken in the morning. It should continue until you fall asleep. What is important is that you keep watchful, whether you are working or sitting or going to the bathroom."

Posture and concentration are related. Often drowsiness (in meditation or at any time) is a clue that your posture has slipped and that your lungs are not able to fill fully with each breath. In such instances, quietly adjust, rolling up from the base of the spine in order to lengthen it and maximize room for breathing. Then take a few deep breaths. The goal is to create maximum room for breath to flow unimpeded. Posture and mood are related as well. When you notice that your mood is sour, try changing your posture.

The word *upright* can refer to posture, but it can also describe how we live our life. "Upright" implies living with integrity, virtue, and steadfastness. Whatever life brings to us, we are not knocked off our foundation. Our life is aligned in all its aspects. The Buddha is often called the Noble One, not because he was born a prince but because he practiced meditation and mindfulness diligently, becoming a person who lived in full alignment with underlying Truth. Through practice we, too, can be infused with this Truth and let it inspire, support, and guide our lives.

When we focus on our breath, we uncover our inherent equanimity. When we allow the churning thoughts in our mind to settle, we discover our inherent wisdom. When we relax and open our hearts, our innate kindness emerges. When we have practiced long enough to be able to access these qualities at any time, we will move through life with confidence, upright and unshakeable.

**Final Words:** Body and mind are not two—they are deeply connected and interdependent. When the mind or mood slumps, try adjusting the body's posture.

# 8

# Gratitude at the End of the Day

The Exercise: At the end of the day, write a list of at least five things that happened during the day that you are grateful for. At the end of the week, read it out loud to a friend, partner, or mindfulness companion.

### REMINDING YOURSELF

Keep a notepad and pencil or pen beside your bed or on your pillow. When you get into bed at night, write your list before you lie down and fall asleep.

### DISCOVERIES

When people first do this practice, they often think that they will have trouble making a list of at least five things they are grateful for. However, they are surprised to find that when they start, the list often grows longer. It is as if a long-neglected faucet were turned on, and the flow doesn't shut off. During the day you may find yourself taking mental notes of "things to add to the list." This encourages a lovely transformation into a mind-state of ongoing gratitude.

Research conducted by Lywbomirsky shows that 40 percent of happiness is determined by our intentional activities. People who keep a daily "gratitude journal" or who regularly express gratitude to people who have been kind to them show a significant increase in happiness and decrease in depression.

We may know people who are naturally grateful. To be around them lifts our spirits and brightens the day. The Buddha spoke of "cultivating" the mind, letting unwholesome emotions and thoughts wither away while strengthening wholesome ones. How is this possible? It is an energetic phenomenon. Anything that is fed energy will grow. It may seem artificial at first, but when we deliberately cultivate gratitude, we will gradually become naturally grateful people. (Conversely, if we cultivate negative mind-states, jealousy, or criticism, they will become who we are.)

DEEPER LESSONS

Our mind seems to be magnetically attracted to the negative. It drags up difficult memories and chews on them, over and over. It keeps trying to change the outcome. "If only I had done that, then he would have . . ." The past is gone. We cannot change its outcome, except by changing ourselves, and that can only be done in the present. The mind thinks up dreadful things that might occur in the future. "What if the economy collapses and there isn't enough food, and people come to our door with guns . . . ?" The mind thinks that it is doing its job, protecting us from danger, but it is actually making us more fearful and tense.

The mind says, "Who cares about the positive things that have happened or will happen? Positive things can't hurt you. My job is to think of all the possible bad outcomes." The news media know this. That is why most news stories have a negative content: "Watch out for this new danger!" "This terrible thing is happening right now, or could happen at any minute!" These are the kinds of stories that the modern mind wants to read, and it makes us buy, read, or listen to them. However, this obsession with the negative can become pervasive, creating an anxious and depressed state of mind. What we expect, namely suffering, becomes what we actually get, a sad self-fulfilling and self-created prophecy.

The practice of gratitude at the end of the day is one antidote to this mental habit of disaster-mongering. This exercise helps us bring to light the many positive and supportive occurrences of the day. It turns the mind-stream in a positive direction. People who practice gratitude at the end of the day regularly find that they become able to see the upside of almost every event in their lives.

---

**Final Words:** Turn the unhappy mind toward discovering even one thing it can be grateful for.

---

# 9

# Listen to Sounds

The Exercise: Several times a day, stop and just listen. Open your hearing 360 degrees, as if your ears were giant radar dishes. Listen to the obvious sounds, and the subtle sounds—in your body, in the room, in the building, and outside. Listen as if you had just landed from a foreign planet and didn't know what was making these sounds. See if you can hear all sounds as music being played just for you.

REMINDING YOURSELF

Post a simple drawing of an ear in various places in your home and workplace.

DISCOVERIES

We are continuously bathed in sound, even in places we would call quiet, such as libraries or forests. Our ears register all these sounds, but our brain blocks most of them out so that we can concentrate on the important ones—the conversation, the lecture, the radio program, the airplane engine, and is that the baby crying?

Research indicates that babies can hear things adults cannot. Their hearing is acute enough to detect the subtle echoes that occur after most sounds. We learn early in life to block these confusing sounds out. Interestingly, African Bushmen retain this ability, probably because they live in the very quiet environment of the desert. Babies also recognize music and the melodic qualities of the voices they heard before birth.

When we begin listening carefully, a new world opens up. Sounds that were annoying become interesting and even amusing when we hear them as some kind of alien music. Background noise moves into the foreground. We discover a lot of noise in our mouth when we eat, especially crunchy food. The neighbor's leaf blower becomes part of the ongoing symphony of sounds. A jackhammer is the percussion section. The hum of the refrigerator unfolds into a tapestry of many subtle high and low notes.

## DEEPER LESSONS

Listening practice is a potent way to quiet the mind. When we become intrigued by sounds, we want to listen more closely. To listen intently, we have to ask the voices in the mind to be quiet for a while. We have to ask the mind not to name ("John's old truck") or talk about the sounds ("He needs a new muffler"), but just to be alert and to listen, as if we were hearing each sound for the first time. In fact, we are. Each sound is just that, completely new.

Listening is an excellent way to disengage from the endless ruminations of the anxious mind. As soon as you find your mind spinning in a squirrel cage of its own making, stop and listen to the music of the room. When you are frazzled after spending an entire day on your computer, step outside, open your awareness out into the darkness, and listen to the music of the evening.

There is a famous koan about sound. A koan is a question for opening the mind into a direct experience of deeper reality. The eminent Japanese Zen master Hakuin assigned his students the koan, "What is the sound of one hand?" It has become trivialized in modern times (and incorrectly repeated as "What is the sound of one hand clapping?"), but when it is taken on with all earnestness, it can open the mind into profound listening.

Reduce this koan to its essence, "What is the sound?" or just "Sound?" When your mind has wandered away down its endless twisting corridors, let this question bring it back to here and now.

---

Final Words: Even in what is called silence there is sound. To hear such subtle sound, the mind must be very quiet.

---

## 10

# Every Time the Phone Rings

The Exercise: Each time you hear a telephone ring, chime, or buzz, stop what you are doing and take three mindful breaths to settle the mind before answering. (If you are a receptionist, you may need to shorten this to one or two breaths. The point is to pause and take at least one deep, cleansing breath before answering the call of the bell.)

If you get very few calls a day on your telephone, set an alarm to ring several times a day, using a long but unusual interval, such as every fifty-three minutes. When the alarm rings, stop and breathe.

REMINDING YOURSELF

Put a colored sticker, or a little note that says "Breathe," on your phone in a place that you will notice every time you pick it up or flip it open to respond to a call.

## DISCOVERIES

We were inspired to try this practice when a large group of students of the Vietnamese Zen monk Thich Nhat Hanh came to our monastery to do a retreat. They have a strong practice of observing mindfulness bells, which are rung at unpredictable intervals throughout the day. Whenever a bell sounded, a wave of silence swept over the room. It didn't matter what people were doing—teaching a class, engaging in conversation, running the dishwasher, serving food—each person stopped talking and stopped moving for the count of three breaths.

Each time a bell rang, all the humming of people's activity just *stopped*. You could feel the energy in the room settle and re-establish itself in a place of more stability and presence. One person noticed, "I saw two people having an intense discussion when the mindfulness bell rang. They stopped mid-sentence, their faces visibly softened, and then they smiled at each other."

Most people automatically reach for the phone when it rings, answering it as soon as possible. It is difficult at first to interrupt this habit, to pause and breathe. Taking a few mindful breaths when the telephone rings is a very practical and useful new habit to cultivate, especially if your job requires you to talk to difficult people, people who are carrying a big load of mental or emotional pain and who want to off-load some of it onto you. It helps you encounter each client, customer, or patient with a clear mind and open heart. A receptionist said, "I'm learning to wait until the third ring of the telephone. It's an opportunity to stop what I'm thinking or doing and compose myself. I practice emptying my mind so that I can give full attention to the person who's calling."

An emergency-room nurse said, "I'm used to working fast and continuously. I resented the mindfulness bell at first. I was weeding in the greenhouse, and I didn't like having to stop my work, even briefly. But then I noticed the deep red color of the chard stems around me, the light shining through their stems. It was beautiful." It was beauty he would have missed, beauty that we all miss, when we are caught up in our busy minds, only partially present, looking but not *really looking*.

### DEEPER LESSONS

This is a powerful task because it invokes sudden stillness in the body and sudden stillness in the mind at the same time. When we are moving, we are usually thinking. When the body stops, a subtle level of ongoing thinking is revealed. Seeing it, we are able to let it go and open to deeper levels of quiet in the mind. One young man noticed a dual benefit in this task. Stopping moving and talking helped him drop mental tension, while enjoying three mindful breaths helped him release physical tension.

One woman said that this task made her anxious at first. She soon realized that the anxiety was not related to how well she was doing the exercise, but was an underlying, low-level anxiety that was always present, unrelated to anything that was happening. She then began to use the interval of three breaths to breathe out a phrase of loving-kindness—"May I be at ease"—which helped dispel her anxiety.

So much of our life is lived unconsciously and in haste. What are we rushing toward? Instead of living fully in this moment, we are always moving forward, grabbing at the next minute, the next hour, the next day. We drag our state of mind, like a bag of garbage, from one encounter to the next. If we've just hung up on a difficult phone call, we're likely to be grumpy with the hapless person who calls us next. To answer each phone call fresh, without the clouding emotions of impatience, anxiety, or irritation, we need to slow things down. We hear the ring, we pause to take one to three breaths, we let go of what is held in the body, heart, and mind. Then we can meet the new caller and new situation with openness and clarity.

We begin by training to do this with ringers or bells as reminders. Eventually the habit spreads to infiltrate the rest of our life. It becomes a new way of being, to be able to let go of what is in our mind and arrive fresh to every encounter throughout the day. This is an extremely useful skill, one that most people do not have. It enables us to let old and harmful habits wither as we cultivate new and healthy ones.

Final Words: Taking three breaths when the phone rings is like a time-out for adults. It's a pause that refreshes.

# 11

# Loving Touch

---

**The Exercise:** Use loving hands and a loving touch, even with inanimate objects.

---

REMINDING YOURSELF

Put something unusual on a finger of your dominant hand. Some possibilities include a different ring, a Band-Aid, a dot of nail polish on one nail, or a small mark made with a colored pen. Each time you notice the marker, remember to use loving hands, loving touch.

DISCOVERIES

When we do this practice, we soon become aware of when we or others are not using loving hands. We notice how groceries are thrown into the shopping cart, luggage is hurled onto a conveyor belt at the airport, and silverware is tossed into a bin.

We hear metal bowls singing out when stacked carelessly and doors slamming when we rush.

A particular dilemma arose at our monastery for people who were weeding the garden. How can we practice loving hands when we are pulling a living plant out of the ground by its roots? Can we keep our heart open to it, placing it in the compost with a prayer that its life (and ours) will benefit others?

As a medical student, I worked with a number of surgeons who were known for their "surgical temperament." If any difficulty arose during an operation, they would act like two-year-olds, throwing expensive instruments and cursing at nurses. I noticed that one surgeon was different. He remained calm under stress, but more importantly, he handled the tissue of each unconscious patient as if it were precious. I resolved that if I needed surgery, I would insist he do it.

As we do this practice, mindfulness of loving touch expands to include awareness not just of how we touch things, but awareness also of how we are touched. This includes not just how we are touched by human hands, but also how we are touched by our clothing, the wind, the food and drink in our mouth, the floor under our feet, and many other things.

We know how to use loving hands and touch. We touch babies, faithful dogs, crying children, and lovers with tenderness and care. Why don't we use loving touch all the time? This is the essential question of mindfulness. Why can't I live like this all the time? Once we discover how much richer our life is when we are more present, why do we fall back into our old habits and space out?

We are being touched all the time, but we are largely unaware of it. Touch usually only enters our awareness when it is uncomfortable (a rock in my sandal) or associated with intense desire (when she or he kisses me for the first time). When we begin to open our awareness to all the touch sensations, both inside and outside of our bodies, we might feel frightened. It can be overwhelming.

Ordinarily we are more aware of using loving touch with people than with objects. However, when we are in a hurry or upset with someone, we turn him or her into an object. We rush out of the house without saying good-bye to someone we love, we ignore a coworker's greeting because of a disagreement the day before. This is how other people become objectified, a nuisance, an obstacle, and ultimately, an enemy.

In Japan objects are often personified. Many things are honored and treated with loving care, things we would consider inanimate and therefore not deserving of respect, let alone love. Money is handed to cashiers with two hands, tea whisks are given personal names, broken sewing needles are given a funeral and laid to rest in a soft block of tofu, the honorific "o-" is attached to mundane things such as money (o-kane), water (o-mizu), tea (o-cha), and even chopsticks (o-hashi). This may come from the Shinto tradition of honoring the kami or spirits that reside in waterfalls, large trees, and mountains. If water, wood, and stone are seen as holy, then all things that arise from them are also holy.

My Zen teachers taught me, through example, how to handle all things as if they were alive. Zen master Maezumi Roshi opened envelopes, even junk mail, using a letter opener in order to make a clean cut, and removed the contents with careful attention. He became upset when people used their feet to drag meditation cushions around the floor or banged their plates down on the table. "I can feel it in my body," he once said. While most modern priests use clothes hangers, Zen master Harada Roshi takes time to fold his monk's robes each night, and to "press" them under his mattress or suitcase. His everyday robe is always crisp. There are robes hundreds of years old in his care. He treats each robe as the robe of the Buddha.

Can we imagine the touch-awareness of enlightened beings? How sensitive and how wide might their field of awareness be? Jesus became immediately aware when a sick woman touched the hem of his garment was been healed.

---

**Final Words:** "When you handle rice, water, or anything else, have the affectionate and caring concern of a parent raising a child." —Zen master Dogen

---

## 12

# Waiting

---

The Exercise: Any time you find yourself waiting—
when you're in line at the store, waiting for someone
who's late, or waiting for the "please wait" icon on your
computer screen to go away—take this as an opportunity
to practice mindfulness, meditation, or prayer.

---

There are several good mindfulness practices for waiting
time. One is mindfulness of breath, beginning with a few
deep breaths to help dispel body tension over having to wait
or the possibility of someone you are waiting for being late.
Find the place in your body where you are most aware of the
breath—nostrils, chest, or belly—and put your attention on
the sensations in that area, noticing how they are continuously
changing.

Another useful practice for waiting time is listening to
sounds, opening and expanding your hearing to take in the
whole room. Other good practices include loving-kindness for
the body (chapter 51) and relaxing on the out-breath: each

time you breathe out, notice any extra holding or tension in the body—around the eyes or mouth, in the shoulders or belly—and let it soften.

When you notice yourself becoming annoyed by having to "wait," remind yourself, "This is terrific! I have some unexpected time to practice mindfulness."

### REMINDING YOURSELF

Put a small note or piece of tape with the letter *W* (for "waiting practice") on the timing devices you check throughout the day, such as your watch, the clock in your car, or your cell phone. Also put a *W* on your computer screen or mouse.

### DISCOVERIES

I discovered this practice when I was new to meditation, working seventy-two-hour weeks as an intern at a busy county hospital, with barely enough time to go to the bathroom. Two Zen teachers came by to visit me at the hospital. I hurried into the waiting room, murmuring apologies for keeping them waiting. "No problem," one said. "It gave us some extra time to sit." ("Sit" is Zen slang for doing sitting meditation.) Oh, yes.

This practice answers the question "When can I—a very busy person—find time to practice mindfulness?" We don't need to dedicate a large block of time to mindfulness practice (though that certainly doesn't hurt). Opportunities to practice being present arise throughout the day.

When we are forced to wait, say in a traffic jam, our instinct is to do something to distract ourselves from the discomfort of waiting. We turn on the radio, call or text someone on the phone, or just sit and fume. Practicing mindfulness while waiting helps people find many small moments in the day when they can bring the thread of awareness up from where it lies hidden in the complex fabric of their lives. Waiting, a common event that usually produces negative emotions, can be transformed into a gift, the gift of free time to practice. The mind benefits doubly: first, by abandoning negative mind-states, and second, by gaining the beneficial effects of even a few extra minutes of practice woven into the day.

My original "waiting practice" teacher was my very patient father. On Sunday morning he would don a suit and tie, and then get into the car to read the Sunday paper. Meanwhile his wife and three daughters would get into the car, one by one, and then get out again to run back and forth on many trips to retrieve gloves, pocketbooks, lipsticks, socks without holes, barrettes, Sunday school books, and so on. Only when the running and slamming of doors ceased would he look up, calmly fold the paper, and start the engine.

### DEEPER LESSONS

As you undertake this practice, you learn to recognize early the body changes that accompany impending negative thoughts and emotions such as impatience about having to wait, or anger about "that idiot" ahead of us in the checkout line. Each time we are able to stop and not allow a negative mind-state to come to fruition (say, getting irritated at the traffic or angry at the slow cashier), we are erasing a habitual and unwholesome pattern of the heart/mind. If we don't let the cart of the mind keep running down the same deep ruts, down the same old hill, into the same old swamp, eventually the ruts will fill in.

Eventually our habitual states of irritation and frustration over something like waiting will dissolve. It takes time, but it works. And it's worth it, as everyone around us will benefit.

Many of us have a mind that measures self-worth in terms of productivity. If I did not produce anything today, if I did not write a book, give a speech, bake bread, earn money, sell something, buy something, get a good grade on a test, or find my soul mate, then my day was wasted and I am a failure. We give ourselves no credit for taking "being"-time, for just being present. "Waiting" is thus a source of frustration. Think of the things I could be getting done!

And yet, if you asked the people you care about what they would like most from you, their answer is likely to be some version of "your presence" or "your loving attention." Presence has no measurable product except positive feelings, feelings of support, intimacy, and happiness. When we stop being busy and productive and switch to just being still and aware, we ourselves will also feel support, intimacy, and happiness, even if no one else is around. These positive feelings are a "product" that is much desired but that cannot be bought. They are the natural result of presence. They are a birthright that we have forgotten we have.

---

Final Words: Don't be annoyed when you have to wait; rejoice in extra time to practice being present.

---

## 13

# A Media Fast

The Exercise: For one week, do not take in any media. This includes news media, social media, and entertainment. Do not listen to the radio, iPod, or CDs; don't watch TV, films, or videos; don't read newspapers, books, or magazines (whether online or in print form); don't surf the Internet; and don't check on social media sites such as Facebook and Twitter.

You don't have to plug your ears if someone tells you about a news event, but do avoid being drawn into a conversation about the news. If people insist, tell them about your unusual fast. You may, of course, do reading that is necessary for work or school.

What to do instead? Part of this mindfulness practice is discovering alternatives to consuming media. Hint: do something with your own hands and your own body.

## REMINDING YOURSELF

Cover the TV with a sheet, or put a sign on your car radio and computer screen reminding you "No News or Entertainment This Week." Let magazines accumulate and consider putting any newspapers you subscribe to straight into the recycling bin. You would do this if you went on vacation—why not now?

## DISCOVERIES

I invented this task for a student who suffered from a very common problem—chronic, low-level anxiety. At the end of a six-day silent retreat he shared with me his happiness over his calm state of mind. An hour later, at lunch, however, I heard him fuming, as usual, about the terrible state the world was in. An admitted "news junkie" who grew up in New York City, he undertook a media fast with great reluctance.

He discovered that his state of mind was good upon arising, and while doing his early-morning meditation. But as soon as the meditation ended, his habit was to grab a cup of coffee and turn on the morning news, "So I can see how the b*!tards have messed up now." During the media fast he was surprised to find that if he wasn't up on the latest news, it didn't really matter, at home or at work. He was, however, experiencing a much calmer state of mind, as was his patient wife.

One difficulty during "withdrawal" is finding an activity to substitute for the time usually spent with the media. You can meditate, take a walk, play a game with your family, cook something from scratch, weed the garden, take photos, do artwork, learn a new language or how to play a musical instrument, or just sit on the porch and relax.

You might discover that not knowing the latest news makes you feel powerless, lazy, or stupid. People ask me, "What if something important happens, such as a fire or a terrorist bombing?" I say, "Don't worry, if it's that important, someone will tell you about it."

### DEEPER LESSONS

For the first two hundred thousand years of human history, we were only exposed to the news (and the suffering) of those immediately around us in our tribes and villages. We saw birth, sickness, death, and wars, but on a limited scale. Only in the last forty years or so has the news media poured the suffering of the entire world—wars, natural disasters, torture, starvation—into our ears and eyes every day, day after day. This suffering that we are helpless to fix accumulates in our mind and heart, and makes us suffer in turn. When the mind and heart become too full of pictures of violence, destruction, and pain, we must take time to empty ourselves.

A media fast is one way to do this. (A silent meditation retreat is even better.)

People who work with trauma victims are known to suffer from something called "secondary victimization." They are affected by the trauma, too, even though they are only hearing about it and did not experience it firsthand. Since the invention of TV and the nightly news, all of us suffer to a certain degree from secondary victimization, caused by the incessant flow of vivid images out of the screen and into our mind—images of murder, genocide, earthquakes, and deadly epidemics. This constant bombardment creates chronic anxiety and makes us heartsick. The world is flawed, millions of innocent people suffer, and we are unable to do much to change it.

If we can decrease our intake of these toxic images, we can more easily establish a heart that is open and a mind that is serene and clear. This is the best foundation we can have if we want to move out into the world of woe and make a positive difference.

---

Final Words: A steady diet of negative news makes the mind ill. Give the mind the good medicine of silence, beauty, and loving friendship.

---

# 14

# Loving Eyes

The Exercise: This week, endeavor to look at things and people with loving eyes. Notice any changes that occur in your eyes, face, body, heart/mind, visual field, and focus when you remember to look with loving eyes.

## REMINDING YOURSELF

Find or create some images of eyes, perhaps eyes with a heart for a pupil. Post these in various places around the house, such as on the bathroom mirror, on the refrigerator, on the back of your front door.

## DISCOVERIES

We know how to use loving eyes when we are falling in love, when we see a new baby or a cute animal. Why do we not use loving eyes more often? Doing this practice, we find that our usual way of looking at things is not loving. It is either neutral or somewhat negative and critical. We walk into a room and the first thing we notice is that the rug needs vacuuming. Or we greet a family member in the morning, and, instead of pausing to look him in the eye with love, we brush by, avoiding each other's gaze and say something like, "You've got some toothpaste on your cheek," or "Is that what you're wearing today?"

We may love each other, but we forget to show it with our eyes. People often feel more comfortable, and, curiously, more intimate, when they communicate indirectly, by phone or by e-mail. I heard a teenager say that if he has something to tell his girlfriend that might be difficult to talk about, he would rather send a text message and wait for her text reply than talk to her in person. He said, "Sometimes it's hard to talk face-to-face." Intimacy is what we desire, but it also makes us uncomfortable. (Is this why the mind slips off the present moment so often when we are meditating? Is there too much presence in the present moment?)

When people try looking at the world with loving eyes, they report a shift in how they see objects and other people. Their focus often becomes clearer and they notice small details, as if they are looking through a magnifying lens. Some people find the opposite, that their vision is softer or a bit blurred. The visual field may change, becoming narrower or larger. Using loving eyes seems to soften the whole face and bring a slight smile to the lips. The heart/mind opens and critical thoughts melt away.

DEEPER LESSONS

There is a range of different "eyes" that we use, from angry eyes, to critical eyes, to impersonal eyes, to personal eyes, to kind eyes, to loving eyes. The eyes we choose to use will color our perception of the world, changing it from hostile to welcoming. The beings we are looking at are sensitive to which eyes we are using. The eyes we choose to use will have an effect upon our own happiness and the happiness of those beings we are looking at. To know ourselves is to know what kind of eyes we are seeing with and to be able to use these eyes skillfully.

There are five types of eyes described in Buddhist teaching. The first is the human eye. This "eye" gives us an image that we persist in regarding as complete and true, even though the visible light that we can perceive is only a very narrow portion of the electromagnetic spectrum. Insects and other animals perceive phenomena of light and patterns in nature that we cannot see. The second "eye" is the divine eye, which looks down, as if from heaven, and sees humankind within the constant flux of all creation. We sometimes get to see through this second eye, as for example when we meditate or when we look through a telescope, for then we get a glimpse of our true place in the universe, a tiny and brief spark in the immensity of time and change.

The third "eye" is called the wisdom eye. If we could see the molecules that make up our "self," we would see ourselves as bits of energy zinging around in empty space, surrounded by other temporary clusters of energy in an empty space that has no beginning or end. When we are able to quiet the mind in meditation and then look inward for direct evidence of a "self," all we can find are bits of sensation, warmth and coolness, pressure, and movement (which is actually a group of sensations that seem to occur in sequence), plus sensations in the mind that we call "thoughts" and sensations in the body that we call "emotions." When thoughts cease, even briefly, the "glue" that holds this tangle of sensation together dissolves and we can see the self for what it truly is, a mass of sensations floating in empty space.

The fourth "eye" is called the dharma eye. It sees all phenomena, each one unique and precious, emerging from emptiness, existing for a while, and then dissolving again. One who sees through this eye is called a saint or a bodhisattva—one who feels compassion for those who suffer needlessly, and is moved to help them.

The fifth "eye" is the Buddha eye. It combines the views of all other eyes, developed to the highest degree, far beyond our imagination.

When we practice loving eyes, we catch a glimpse through the fourth eye, the eye of the bodhisattva. Seeing with loving eyes is not a one-way experience, nor is it just a visual experience. When we touch something with loving eyes, we bring a certain warmth from our side, but we also may be surprised to feel warmth radiating back to us. We begin to wonder, is everything in the world made of love? And have I been blocking that out?

---

Final Words: Loving eyes can create a loving universe.

---

## 15

# Secret Acts of Virtue

---

**The Exercise**: Each day for a week, engage in a secret act of virtue or kindness. Do something nice or needed for others, but do so anonymously. These acts can be very simple, like washing someone else's dishes that were left in the sink, picking up trash on the sidewalk, cleaning the bathroom sink (when it's not your job), making an anonymous donation, or leaving a chocolate on a coworker's desk.

---

REMINDING YOURSELF

Place a notebook on your bedside table and use it to make a plan each night for what your secret act of virtue will be the next day. You could also post little pictures of elves in strategic places in your home or workplace as reminders.

## DISCOVERIES

It's unexpectedly fun to plan and do nice things in secret for others. Once you take on this task in earnest, you begin looking around for new ideas, and the possibilities begin to multiply. "Oh, tomorrow I could have a cup of hot tea waiting on her desk, or I could clean the mud off his running shoes on the porch." It's like being a superhero named Secret Virtue, who, in the dark of night, creeps about doing good deeds. There's the excitement of trying not to get caught, and, as some people admitted, there can also be a bit of disappointment at not being caught or acknowledged. Even more interesting is remaining silent as someone else is thanked for the gift we gave anonymously.

All religions value generosity. The Bible says it is more blessed to give than to receive. There are two forms of charity in Islam, obligatory giving to take care of the poor and orphaned, and voluntary giving, such as endowments or scholarships. Obligatory giving purifies the rest of one's earnings and is considered a form of prayer or worship. Voluntary giving in secret is said to have seventy times the value of public giving.

One of my favorite practices is what I call "drive-by metta." (Metta is a Pali word meaning loving-kindness, or unconditional friendliness. It also refers to a meditative practice for developing those qualities.) As I drive to work, for each person I pass on the road—pedestrians, bikers, and especially rude drivers who are in a hurry—I say quietly, with my out-breath, "May you be free from anxiety. May you be at ease." I don't know if this secret practice helps them, but it definitely helps me. The days I do drive-by metta always go more easily.

DEEPER LESSONS

Our personality is cobbled together out of many strategies for making others love and care for us, for getting what we want, and for keeping ourselves safe. We bask in positive recognition, for it signals love, success, and security. This task helps us look at how willing we are to put the effort out to do good things for others if we never earn credit for it. Zen practice emphasizes "going straight on"—leading our lives in a straightforward way based upon what we know to be good practice, undaunted by praise or criticism.

A monk once asked the Chinese Zen master Hui-hai, "What is the gate [meaning both entrance and pillar] of Zen practice?" Hui-hai answered, "Complete giving."

The Buddha said, "If people knew, as I know, the fruits of sharing gifts, they would not enjoy their use without sharing them, nor would the taint of stinginess obsess the heart. Even if it were their last bit, their last morsel of food, they would not enjoy its use without sharing it if there was someone else to share it with."

The Buddha spoke constantly of the value of generosity, saying it is the most effective way to reach enlightenment. He recommended giving simple gifts, pure water to drink, food, shelter, clothing, transportation, light, flowers. Even poor people can be generous, he said, by giving a crumb of their food to an ant. Each time we give something away, whether it is a material object or our time (is it "ours"?), we are letting go of a bit of that carefully gathered and fiercely defended temporary heap of stuff we call "I, me, and mine."

**Final Words:** Generosity is the highest virtue, and anonymous giving is the highest form of generosity.

## 16

# Just Three Breaths

**The Exercise:** As many times a day as you are able, give the mind a short rest. For the duration of three breaths ask the inner voices to be silent. It's like turning off the inner radio or TV for a few minutes. Then open all your senses and just be aware—of color, sound, touch, and smell.

REMINDING YOURSELF

Post notes in your environment with the number 3 on them. You could add a drawing of a person with an empty thought balloon above his head. It might help to set an alarm or cell phone to ring at irregular intervals throughout the day.

DISCOVERIES

When people first begin meditating or doing contemplative prayer, they experience a measure of relief from the constantly churning mind. They are happy. If their concentration deepens, however, they are often dismayed to find that their mind is like a hyperactive two-year-old, unable to sit still, at rest in the present moment, for more than a few minutes. It is busy all day long. It journeys to the past, reliving past pleasures and hurts. It darts off into the future, making a hundred plans. It escapes into fantasies, creating imaginary worlds to fulfill all its desires. New meditators also discover their inner voices, which are constantly narrating, comparing and criticizing, rationalizing. At this stage people confess that they are thinking of quitting meditation. Their mind seems noisier than ever! As soon as their mind wanders off the practice, they are filled with self-criticism. Instead of progressing, they seem to be going backward.

It is as if the mind is willing to go along with the game of quieting itself only for a short while. When it realizes that we are quite serious about making it still, and even existing for periods of time without its constant direction, it can panic and begin to spin like a squirrel in a cage. The mind goes into self-protection mode, trying to pinpoint the source of trouble, generating judgment of others and criticism of self. When these negative thoughts and emotions fill the mind, it can undermine and eventually destroy mindfulness practice.

The simple practice of just three breaths can come as a relief. It can interrupt this kind of downward spiral and renew our practice. We ask the mind to rest a bit, to be completely still, just for three breaths. Because we don't have to count three breaths, we can enjoy them. When the three breaths are done, let the mind loose for a bit, then turn its full attention again to just three breaths. As the mind rests more and more in the present moment, it will naturally settle. Then, without effort, we can be present for a few more, and then just a few more breaths, until we are able to sit in relaxed, open awareness.

Even at night our mind does not rest. It creates dreams and processes the undigested material from our days. All this mental activity, all these choices and possibilities, is confusing and even exhausting. Just as the body needs regular rest, so too does the mind.

To rest the mind in complete stillness, in pure awareness, is to return it to its original nature, its natural state. This task helps us break the habit of compulsive thinking. We don't need the mind to narrate all the events of our life. We don't need the mind to comment internally on everything and everyone we encounter. This narration, these comments, separates us from just experiencing life as it is.

The mind has two functions, thinking and awareness. When we are newborn babies, we have no words in our mind. We live in pure awareness. When we learn to speak, words begin to fill our mind and mouth. My two-year-old granddaughter chatters all day long, just to practice her new skill of talking, and she basks in the smiles and praise it brings from adults around her. Learning to talk is a necessary developmental step, but it is also the beginning of a mind that is always speaking inside our heads. This internal talking takes energy. The mind truly rests only when we are able to turn off its thinking function and turn on its awareness function. Usually we wait to do this until we have at least thirty minutes to meditate or center ourselves in prayer. However, we can also sprinkle short moments of mind-rest throughout the day. When our mind does rest, even for a period as short as three breaths, it can become refreshed and clear.

The Buddha talked about the unrestrained mind as a feral

elephant. Its strength is dissipated as it runs around wildly. To harness its power, we must first tie it to a stake. This is what we do when we tie the mind to the breath. Then we teach the elephant to stand still. We teach the mind to empty itself and stand ready, alert but relaxed, waiting for whatever will appear next.

When the mind switches from productive to receptive mode, we return to the pure awareness of infancy. We are able to plug back in to the unlimited Source. Afterward the rejuvenated mind asks, "Why don't we do this more often?"

---

**Final Words:** Prescription for health: Quiet the mind for just three breaths. Repeat as needed.

---

## 17

# Entering New Spaces

---

The Exercise: Our shorthand for this mindfulness practice is "mindfulness of doors," but it actually involves bringing awareness to any transitions between spaces, when you leave one kind of space and enter another. Before you walk through a door, pause, even for a second, and take one breath. Be aware of the differences you might feel in each new space you enter.

Part of this practice is to pay careful attention to how you close the door when entering a new space. We often move immediately into a new space without finishing up with the old one, forgetting to close the door or letting it slam shut.

---

REMINDING YOURSELF

Put an obvious sticker, such as a big star, on the doors you commonly encounter at home. Also remember doors to closets, garages, sheds, basements, and offices. Or you can put a special mark such as a letter D on the back of the hand you use to open doors.

DISCOVERIES

Don't be discouraged if at first you don't succeed in carrying out this task. It is one of the most difficult tasks we've undertaken at the monastery over the years. You find yourself walking toward a door, thinking, "Door. Door. Be mindful walking through the . . ." and suddenly you find yourself on the other side of the door, with no awareness of how you passed through it. After doing this task for a week once or twice a year we have become better at it, eventually becoming aware of entering new spaces even when there wasn't a helpful barrier such as a door.

Differences in spaces are most obvious when you step from indoors to outdoors. There are clear changes in temperature, air quality, smell, light, sound, and even feeling tone. With practice we can also detect these kinds of differences, though they are more subtle, when we enter or exit the many different indoor spaces we move through in a day.

One person used a counter to keep track of the number of doors he passed through—over two hundred forty in one day! That's a lot of potential mindfulness moments. This task seems to spawn creativity and also new tasks. For example, one person added the practice of noticing "doors" in her mind closing and opening as she let go of one train of thought and began another. She became most aware of entering new "rooms" in her mind during meditation. Another person, who had a lifelong habit of slamming doors, worked on closing doors gently. Another tried to make her mind as big as the space in each new room she entered.

It took many of us, including me, several weeks of repeating this task until we were able to bring mindfulness to even half of the doors we walked through. We improved when someone hung a large sheet of Plexiglas in a dim hallway near a commonly used door. We all walked into it several times, even the person who hung it up! A few bangs on the head can do wonders for one's mindfulness.

We also pondered why this exercise was so challenging. One person had an insight: as we walk toward a door, our mind moves ahead to the future, toward what we will be encountering and doing on the other side. This mind movement is not obvious. It takes careful watching. It makes us go unconscious, just briefly, of what we are doing in the present. The unconscious or semiconscious mind, however, is able to steer us through the movements of opening the door and making our way safely through.

This is one example of how we move through much of our day like sleepwalkers, navigating through the world while caught in a dream. This semiconscious state is a source of dissatisfaction (*dukkha* in Sanskrit), the persistent feeling that something is not right, that there is a gap between us and life as it is actually happening. As we learn to become present, bit by bit, the gap closes and life becomes more vivid and satisfying.

---

Final Words: Appreciate each physical space and each mind space that you encounter.

---

## 18

# Notice Trees

The Exercise: During this week become aware of the trees around you. There are many aspects you can attend to, for example, their different shapes (round or slim, neat or shaggy in outline), different heights, ways of branching, and colors and types of foliage. Don't let the mind begin analyzing; just notice and appreciate the trees. (If you live in a treeless area, you can change this to becoming aware of cacti, bushes, or grasses.)

A good time to notice trees is when you are driving or walking, or when you look out windows. If you have a chance, walk among the trees in a park, forest, or tree-lined street. Look at leaves and bark close up. Be aware that trees are breathing. What they breathe out (oxygen), we breathe in. What we breathe out (carbon dioxide), they breathe in.

## REMINDING YOURSELF

Post a small picture of a tree on the dashboard of your car and on windows you often look through.

## DISCOVERIES

Trees can easily become "part of the wallpaper" in our lives. We take their presence for granted and stop seeing them individually and clearly. Once we begin looking actively, we notice that trees are everywhere, and their forms are complex and various. Noticing the many different shades of green in the trees and plants we pass is a wonderful mindfulness task of its own. Painters notice many colors besides brown in the bark of trees, such as purple or orange.

We notice how trees change with the seasons: in spring the delicate chartreuse haze of tiny new leaves; in autumn the yellows, oranges, and reds. In winter we see the skeletons of trees, the many different branching patterns, and the nests of birds or leaf-bundle homes of squirrels that were previously hidden by summer foliage. We become curious and learn the names of trees.

In our forest at the monastery we have a huge bigleaf maple that is about two hundred years old. It is called "the Mansion Maple" because it is home to thousands of creatures, from ferns to chipmunks to centipedes. We can imagine what it has seen passing by in its lifetime—bobcats, shrews and deer, Native Americans, Finnish farmers, and Zen monks in robes.

To restore our connection to trees, each summer at our monastery we have a weeklong silent retreat in which everyone picks a tree in the forest and sits under and with it, both in the daytime and also during the night. Each person learns something important from these hours of communion. Whenever I am working on a tangled mind-problem, I go into the woods and sit down, leaning up against a tree. I merge my awareness with the awareness of the tree, stretching my imagination from the ends of the roots deep in the damp earth to the tips of the topmost leaves blowing about in the breeze. Then I ask for the tree's perspective on my dilemma. It always helps.

## DEEPER LESSONS

Mindfulness of our continuous, inter-breathing relationship with trees and green plants can provide us with vivid awareness of our interconnectedness with all beings. Unless we are a botanist or arborist, it is easy to stop noticing these beneficial and ubiquitous companions. If a living being doesn't catch our notice by being noisy, moving about, looking soulfully into our eyes, or being dangerous, we stop noticing it. If trees disappeared, we would notice it quickly, because we would all become overheated, get sick, and die. One young tree provides the cooling effect of ten room-sized air conditioners. Trees work in tandem with us, taking in the carbon dioxide we breathe out and releasing oxygen. An acre of trees produces four tons of oxygen a year, enough to keep eighteen people happily breathing.

A number of studies have shown that viewing natural environments containing trees for just a few minutes, or even looking at pictures of trees, can lower blood pressure, relax muscle tension, lower levels of fear and anger, reduce pain, ease stress, and shorten recovery time from surgery. We humans evolved over two hundred thousand years in close association with plants and trees. Only in the last few decades have most people been living, working, commuting—in fact, spending the entire day—in sealed boxes. We suffer when we lose our connection to nature's nourishing and healing capacities.

A botanist once came to the monastery to teach us about the plants around us. As he walked around the grounds, he kept exclaiming happily, "Oh, what a huge red huckleberry bush!" "Oh! I've never seen such a big patch of yellow wood violets." I realized that everywhere this man went, his inner experience was that of being among welcoming friends. He was never alone, always in the presence of beings whose very existence gave him joy. I imagine that bird-watchers feel the same way, that is, they are never without lovely companions.

This practice, opening our awareness to all the living beings around us, can be an antidote for the pervasive feeling of loneliness that plagues so many of us. Even in the city there are animals, birds, plants, and insects all around us. Within our bodies are billions of living beings, most of them beneficial. Their lives are intertwined with ours, and they are necessary to our health and we to theirs. When our mind closes down tightly on the worries of "I, me, mine," we create loneliness. When we open our heart into awareness of all those beings we are connected to, our loneliness melts away.

Final Words: Please remember, you are always supported by countless beings, including trees. You are never alone.

## 19

# Rest Your Hands

---

**The Exercise:** Several times a day let your hands relax completely. For at least a few seconds, let them be completely still. One way to do this is to place them in your lap and then focus your awareness on the subtle sensations in the quiet hands.

---

REMINDING YOURSELF

Wear your watch backward. If you don't wear a watch, put a string or rubber band around your wrist.

DISCOVERIES

The hands are always busy. If they are not busy, they are somewhat tense, ready to work.

The hands reveal our state of mental ease or discomfort. Many people have unconscious nervous hand gestures, such as rubbing or wringing their hands, touching their face, tapping a finger, snapping a fingernail, cracking their knuckles, or twiddling their thumbs. When people first learn to meditate, they often have a hard time letting the hands be still. They may restlessly rearrange the position of their hands, and as soon as there is a small itch, the hands fly up to scratch it.

When we relax our hands, the rest of the body and even the mind will relax, too. Relaxing the hands is a way of quieting the mind. We also found that when the hands are quiet in our lap, we can listen more attentively.

As I did this task, I discovered that my hands tighten on the steering wheel when I am driving. Now I can check for this unconscious habit, and relax my grip. I realized that I can hold the wheel with a lighter grip and still drive safely. When I relax my hands on the steering wheel, I often find that ten minutes later, they have resumed their habitual tight grip again. This is why we call it mindfulness "practice." We have to do it over and over again to truly become aware. We set out to do the practice, then revert to unconscious behavior, then become aware again, then start the practice again, and so on.


DEEPER LESSONS

Body and mind work together. When we put the mind at ease, the body can relax. When the body is still, the mind can settle. The health of both is improved.

Tension is not necessary for most of the tasks of our life. It is a waste of energy. There is a meditation called a "body scan" that can first help us to discover unconscious tension lurking in the body and can then help us to soften or dispel it. It goes like this: You sit quietly and focus your awareness on one part of the body at a time, beginning at the top. What are the sensations coming from the scalp and hair? Once you are aware of these sensations, try to notice any extra holding or tension you may be doing and try to gently soften or release it as you breathe out. Next move on to the forehead, then the eyes, and so on, one body part at a time. It is interesting to discover how much tension is unconsciously held, and in which body parts.

We generally go through most of our lives in one of two modes. At night we are lying down, relaxed and asleep. When the alarm clock rings, we get up and switch to the mode we use during the day, upright, holding tension, and alert. There are not many times in our busy lives when we are both upright *and* relaxed. (Unfortunately there are also times when we are lying down and are *neither* relaxed nor asleep. We are instead brooding, anxious, and restlessly shifting, unable to sleep.)

Being awake, alert, and relaxed is a state we may experience on a vacation day. We wake up later than usual, fully rested, and lie in bed a while without anything on our mind or anything to accomplish. We hear the birds and the garbageman, but there is no tension in the body or mind. My mother used to call this "the time in-between, my best time to ponder important things." This is true, it is the best time, because the mind unclouded by worries about the survival of "I, me, and mine" can look more deeply into important matters. In meditation we purposely widen this in-between state. We purposely become relaxed while remaining upright and alert. It isn't easy at first. We tip over into worry that our meditation isn't perfect, that we won't become enlightened. Our shoulders begin to ache with tension. Or we tip over into drowsiness, relaxed and almost falling over, until a noise surprises us awake. It takes us a while to get our balance.

**Final Words:** Remember to relax the hands, and with them, the whole body and mind.

## 20

# Say Yes

---

**The Exercise:** In this practice we say yes to everyone and everything that happens. When you notice the impulse to disagree, consider whether it is really necessary. Could you just nod, or even be silent but pleasant? Whenever it is not dangerous to you or others, agree with others and with what is happening in your life.

---

### REMINDING YOURSELF

Put stickers with the word "Yes" in spots where you'll notice them in your home and workplace. Write "Yes" on the back of your hand so you see it frequently.

### DISCOVERIES

This task helps us see how often we take a stance that is negative or oppositional. If we are able to watch our mind when someone is talking to us, particularly if they are asking us to do something, we can see our thoughts forming defenses and counterarguments. Can we resist the desire to disagree verbally when the issue is not critical? Can we watch our mental and physical attitude to things that arise in a typical day? Is our automatic thought, "Oh no"?

Our habitual oppositional stance can take the form of thoughts ("I don't agree with what he's saying"), body language (tensing muscles, arms crossed), speech ("That's a stupid idea"), or action (shaking the head, rolling the eyes, ignoring someone who's talking).

People in certain professions report that they have difficulty with this task. Lawyers, for example, are trained to detect flaws in a contract or faults in what a witness or another lawyer is saying. Academics are trained to criticize one another's theories and research. Success at work may depend on "attack mind," but when you spend an entire day cultivating this attitude, it can be difficult to turn it off when you arrive home.

While doing this task, one person noted that an external "yes" might not match the real attitude of "no" inside, and that the task helped him detect a hidden constricted state of mind. Another man found that he usually responds to requests by weighing other considerations—namely, all the other things he has to do. He found it freeing to just say yes and thus let go of all the internal effort involved in making a decision. It felt generous. Another person said that saying yes created the experience of ease, of going with the flow of people who came into her office rather than resisting it. This task may be modified according to circumstances. You can hold an inward "yes" to your child's wish to jump on furniture, but redirect their energy to the playground instead.

The Buddhist tradition describes three poisons of the mind—greed, aversion, and ignorance. We developed this task for Zen students who seem particularly afflicted by aversion, those who habitually resist anything asked of them and what comes forward in life. Their initial and unconscious response to anything asked of them is "no," expressed either in body language or out loud. Sometimes the no is expressed as "yes, but . . . ," and sometimes it is cloaked in reasonable language, but it is still a consistent and persistent pattern of opposition.

People who are stuck in aversion often make major life decisions based not upon moving toward a positive goal but rather upon moving away from something they perceive to be negative. They are reactive rather than proactive. "My parents didn't pay their bills on time and our electricity got turned off. I'm going to become an accountant," instead of "I want to become an accountant because I love numbers."

When monks enter training at Japanese Soto Zen monasteries, they are told that the only acceptable response to anything they are asked to do in the first year of training is, "Hai! (Yes!)." This is powerful training. It cuts through layers of apparent maturity, down to the defiant two-year-old and/or teenager within.

Not expressing opposition helps us to let go of self-centered views and see that our personal opinion is actually not so important after all. It's surprising how often our disagreement with another person is actually unimportant and only serves to increase our distress and the suffering of those around us.

Saying yes can be energizing, since habitual resistance is a persistent drain on our life energy.

---

**Final Words:** Cultivate an internal attitude of "yes" to life and all it brings you. It will save you lots of energy.

---

# 21

# See the Color Blue

---

The Exercise: Become aware of the color blue wherever it appears in your environment. Look not just for the obvious instances, such as the sky, but also for subtle appearances and for all variations of blue.

---

## REMINDING YOURSELF

Put a small dot of blue marker on the back of your hand or inside your wrist. Stick little squares of blue paper up around the house where you'll see them, on doors, on the refrigerator, and so on.

When you notice these reminders, pause for a moment to look around you for the color blue. It could be any tint of blue, and any size from a small dot to a large expanse.

It may help to soften your gaze and "invite" the color blue to appear.

## DISCOVERIES

This task was suggested by a student who is an artist and is very aware of colors. When we reported in after a week of doing this task, he explained that he sees blue in every color. Purple, green, brown, and even black shimmer with bits of blue. Most of us found the color blue in many unexpected places. There are so many blues, from subtle to obvious. Softening the gaze brings a luminosity to all colors and forms.

In some languages, the same word is used for both green and blue, or for both black and blue. For example, there is an ancient word and character for blue (*aoi*) in Japanese, but a separate word for green (*midori*) only came into use later, in the Heian period, not appearing in educational materials until the occupation after World War II. In other languages, such as Greek, there are many names for different shades of blue—*thalassi* for sea blue, *ourani* for sky blue, *galzio* for light blue, and so on.

People report that when they remember to look around for the color blue, it seems to pop out at them. Blue objects seem to stand out, as if they have become more three-dimensional. This task also opens up a new appreciation of the sky, the huge bowl of blue that we ignore most of the time even though it is usually a large part of our visual field. The bright blue sky is always above us, even when it is overcast or raining. We realize this when we are flying and the airplane ascends through low-lying clouds and emerges into brilliant sunshine.

## DEEPER LESSONS

When we remember to open our awareness to the color blue, it seems to become more vivid and more omnipresent. Of course, it didn't just become so. It is always sharp and clear. However, it is only when we are mindful that we become aware of its ubiquitous presence in our lives.

How do we know that what I see and call blue is what you are seeing? Each of us lives in our own world, and no one else can enter or experience it fully. The experiences even of identical twins are unique. We are the only one who sees blue as we see it. Similarly, our particular life will never happen again, and we are the only one who can live it fully.

Tibetan Buddhists describe our essential nature as like the sky, vast, luminous, and clear. Meditation helps us reclaim this unbounded mind, which is able to illuminate and see deeply into anything we turn it to. Clearing the mind is similar to our everyday experience with computer screens. We find ourselves completely caught up in the compelling and complex world on the screen. For a while it is our entire reality. Then something pulls us away from the screen—a real person stops by to talk. Our computer screen reverts to a "screen saver," perhaps a photo of a few white clouds in a bright blue sky. Suddenly our awareness expands and we are lifted above the narrow world of one small glowing screenful of words.

When we find ourselves caught up in the compelling and complex inner screen of our mind, we need to remember that we have an option. We can shrink or "minimize" the current screen down to a small icon on the bottom of the mind-screen and open up the serene blue sky of our inherently boundless, clear mind. A few thoughts drift across the screen, like wispy white clouds. We are lifted above the narrow world of "I, me, and mine" to a place of serenity. The small icon of our worries and plans can be opened up whenever we wish.

Just as the blue sky is always above us, even when we cannot see it, so it is with our perfect Original Nature. Even when our mind-state is cloudy and our emotions are raining, our Original Nature is always there, shining brightly within us and all things.

---

**Final Words:** We can break out of the dark and narrow prison of self-absorbed mind and find freedom in the luminous sky mind.

---

## 22

# Bottoms of the Feet

---

The Exercise: As often as possible during the day, place your awareness in the bottoms of your feet. Become aware of the sensations on the bottoms of the feet such as the pressure of the floor or ground beneath the feet, or the warmth or coolness of the feet. It is particularly important to do so whenever you notice yourself becoming anxious or upset.

---

REMINDING YOURSELF

The classic method for remembering this task is to put a small stone in your shoe. A less painful, though probably less effective, way is to place notes that say "Feet" where you'll see them, or cutouts of footprints in appropriate locations on the floor. You could also set your cell phone or timer to ring at certain intervals during the day, and whenever you hear the ringer, turn your awareness to the bottoms of your feet.

DISCOVERIES

Through this mindfulness practice, people noticed that ordinarily they walked about without paying much attention to their feet, unless their feet were hurting or they stumbled. If people were caught up in thinking, moving their awareness from the head to the feet had the effect of settling the mind. This probably occurs because the bottoms of the feet are as far as we can get away from the head, where we often seem to think our "selves" are located. We identify very closely with our thoughts and give our mind/brain an exalted status. Many of us unconsciously view the body merely as a servant of the brain—the body is equipped with feet to transport the commanding mind around, and with hands to get things the mind thinks it wants, such as doughnuts.

We often begin meals at the monastery by sitting in silence and placing our awareness in the bottoms of our feet. It helps to bring mindfulness to eating. We've also found that when we are aware of the bottoms of the feet, our balance improves and we are more sure-footed.

Martial arts and yoga emphasize being aware of the feet and mentally extending a sense of connection or roots down into the earth. This gives rise to both physical stability and mental equanimity. When we become anxious, the mind becomes more active, like a hamster in an exercise wheel, spinning around, trying to figure out how to escape mental or physical discomfort. Doing this task, people discover that when they bring awareness to all the tiny sensations on the bottoms of the feet, the flow of ever-changing physical sensations fills the mind completely and there is no room at all for thinking. They feel less top-heavy, more anchored, less likely to be pushed about by thoughts and emotions. Dropping awareness into the bottoms of the feet clears the mind and lifts clouds of anxiety.

### DEEPER LESSONS

Our mind likes to think. It thinks that if it is not thinking, it is failing at its job of guiding and protecting us. However, when the mind becomes overactive, the opposite occurs. Its guidance becomes shrill, even cruel, and its constant warnings fill us with anxiety. How can we put the thinking mind in its proper place and perspective? We shift the mind from thinking to awareness, beginning with full awareness of the body.

An essential aspect of Zen practice is walking meditation, called kinhin. We do it without shoes so that the sensations on the bottoms of the feet will be maximized. Walking meditation helps bring the quiet body/mind of seated meditation into our ordinary active world. Silent walking is a bridge between one side of meditation—silent sitting in pure awareness—and the other side—speaking and moving about. It is not so easy to keep the mind still while walking. Any movement of the body seems to produce movement of the mind.

We can challenge ourselves. Can I keep my mind still and focused in the bottoms of my feet for one or two circuits around the room? Or for the entire length of an outdoor walking path? Or from here to the corner?

---

**Final Words:** Placing your awareness in the bottoms of your feet will lead to mental stability and emotional serenity, if you practice it diligently.

---

## 23

# Empty Space

---

The Exercise: As often as you can, shift your awareness from objects to the space around the objects. For example, when you look in the mirror, notice the space around the image of your head. In a room, notice the empty space rather than the furniture, people, or other visual objects.

---

REMINDING YOURSELF

Post blank squares of paper, or notes that say "Space," in places where you will see them.

DISCOVERIES

Ordinarily our focus is on objects. Inside a house we focus on the people, animals, furniture, appliances, dishes, and so forth. Outside we still have tunnel vision, focusing on buildings, trees and plants, vehicles, animals, roadways, signs, and people. It takes an effort to shift our awareness to the space around all these objects or within rooms. Opening the mind to this space is somehow restful. Is our anxiety linked to objects?

This task can be a potent tool of awareness if people consistently practice with it. One student commented that ikebana, the Japanese art of flower arranging, helped her appreciate space. "I am learning to see space, which is as important as the objects in the space. Space keeps everything from being jumbled together and helps reveal the beauty of the leaves, branches, and flowers." Similarly, space in our mind keeps everything from being covered over with a jumble of thoughts and reveals the simplicity and beauty of everything we see. Another person added, "When I looked at the space around an object, it suddenly 'popped' out and became more vivid. I also saw how chairs and many other things function only because of their empty space." Another said, "It was as if everything was continuous, connected by space, and that everything was in meditation with me."

Tears glistened in the eyes of one person as he described his experience. "When I remembered to be aware of space, it was as if the walls expanded and there was more space around everything. I decided to apply this to my thoughts, and suddenly there was space around them, too. My sense of 'I am' fell away—it was just a thought held in a field of space. But then my mind said, 'Wow!' and the heavy sense of self reassembled again." Another person was startled to find space around her emotions and to realize that she is neither her thoughts nor her emotions.

DEEPER LESSONS

Our identity is bound up in objects, objects that reinforce our sense of self. "I'm a book collector," "I have the latest entertainment center," "I have beautiful art on my walls," "I have five cats." All day long we spend time engaging with objects. Our desire is focused on the things, animals, and people we want to occupy the space around us. We seldom step back and see the background, the empty space that makes up most of a room, a building, or an outdoor vista. When we are able to shift our awareness to the space around objects, there is a sense of relief.

It is equally important to perceive the space that exists within the mind. When we can let go of thoughts and hold our awareness on the mind-ground behind the thoughts, there is an immediate feeling of relief. Our suffering is bound up in objects, in the desire to obtain them, keep them, change them, or get rid of them. Any time we find ourselves holding tightly to objects, whether they are physical objects or mental objects such as thoughts and emotions, we are grasping the seeds of suffering. If we can release that hold, reverse our focus, and become aware of the background of emptiness, of possibilities, we can prevent distress and sorrow from growing within us.

Some Christian mystics call God the Ground of Being. To rest in this ground feels like finding our way back home. This is the awareness we had before our birth and in the few months after we were born, before words, then ideas, and then emotions began to fill and cloud the mind. Meditation and prayer still the mind and bring us back to this original ground.

---

Final Words: Let the mind become spacious. Do not be distracted or fooled by its content.

---

## 24

# One Bite at a Time

---

**The Exercise:** This is a mindfulness practice to do whenever you are eating. After you take a bite, put the spoon or fork back down in the bowl or on the plate. Place your awareness in your mouth until that one bite has been enjoyed and swallowed. Only then pick up the utensil and take another bite. If you are eating with your hands, put the sandwich, apple, or cookie down between bites.

---

REMINDING YOURSELF

Post notes with "One Bite at a Time" wherever you eat, or an icon of a spoon or fork with the words "Put It Down!"

DISCOVERIES

This is one of the most challenging mindful-eating practices we do at our monastery. In attempting this exercise, most people discover that they have the habit of "layering" bites of food. That is, they put one bite in the mouth, divert their attention away from the mouth as they shovel food onto the fork or spoon for the next bite, then put a second bite in the mouth before the first one is swallowed. Often the hand is hovering in the air, with another bite halfway to the mouth, as the preceding bite is chewed. They discover that as soon as the mind wanders, the hand assumes control again, putting new bites of food in on top of partially processed bites. It is amazing how hard this simple task can be. It takes time, patience, persistence, and a sense of humor to change long-term habits.

The absorption of food can begin in the mouth, if we chew our food well and let it mix with saliva, which contains digestive enzymes. The earlier absorption begins, the earlier the satiation signals are sent out to the brain, and the sooner we feel full. The sooner we feel full, the more appropriate we can be about the amounts of food we serve ourselves and then consume.

Putting down your utensil between bites used to be part of good manners. It counteracts the tendency to wolf down our food. One person exclaimed after trying this task, "I just realized that I never chew my food. I swallow it almost whole, in my haste to get the next bite in!" She had to ask herself, "Why am I in such a rush to get through a meal, when I enjoy eating so much?"

DEEPER LESSONS

This is actually a task about becoming aware of impatience. Eating quickly, layering one bite on top of another, is a specific example of impatience. Doing this task may lead you to watch the arising of impatience in other aspects and occasions in your life. Do you get impatient when you have to wait? We have to ask ourselves, "Why am I in such a rush to get through life, when I want to enjoy it so much?"

Experiencing one bite or one swallow at a time is a way of experiencing one moment at a time. Since we eat or drink at least three times a day, this mindfulness tool gives us several built-in opportunities to bring mindfulness into each day. Eating is naturally pleasurable, but when we eat quickly and without mindfulness, we don't experience that pleasure. Research shows that, ironically, people eat their favorite foods more quickly than foods they dislike! Binge eaters also report that they keep on eating in an effort to re-create the pleasure of the first bite. Because the taste receptors tire quickly, this can never work.

When the mind is absent, thinking about the past or future, we are only half tasting our food. When our awareness rests in the mouth, when we are fully present as we eat, when we slow our eating down, pausing between bites, then each bite can be like the first, rich and full of interesting sensations.

Pursuing pleasure without mindfulness is like being caught on a treadmill. Mindfulness allows pleasure to bloom in thousands of small moments in our life.

---

Final Words: There can be no party in the mouth if the mind is not invited to attend.

---

## 25

# Endless Desires

---

The Exercise: As often as possible during the day, become aware of the arising of desire.

---

### REMINDING YOURSELF

Post small notes in strategic locations that ask, "What Is My Desire Right Now?"

### DISCOVERIES

People report that prior to doing this exercise they always thought of desire in regard to food or sex. However, as one man reported, after maintaining an awareness of desire throughout the day, he found that desire is constantly arising, from the time he awakens until the final conscious moment before he falls asleep. When the alarm clock rings, desire for more sleep. Walking into the kitchen, desire for coffee. In the evening, desire to lie down in bed. And so on. Many people are stunned to find they are a mass of desire, thinly disguised as "rationality."

The tyranny of desire takes hold very early in life. A half hour after breakfast my two-year-old granddaughter will be outside, swinging happily in her swing, when suddenly her little face screws up into a frown and she declares, "I want ice cream!" A little later it will be "I want chocolate raisins!" She has also learned that "I need . . ." is more potent in getting her desires met than "I want . . . ." She is so transparent, you can watch the clouds of desire pass through and darken her sunny mind. It can take a lot of adult determination and wiles to distract and untangle her from the tentacles of desire.

We all know how desire can take hold of us like a cocklebur. We are not much different from a toddler. We could be walking contentedly through the mall, and suddenly we smell cinnamon buns. We can watch desire arise and begin to nag, negotiate, and rationalize in our mind. It takes determination to stop the internal argument and switch the mind-stream to something healthier.


DEEPER LESSONS

There is nothing innately wrong with desire. Desire keeps us alive. If we had no desire for food, drink, or sleep, we would soon die. If we had no desire for sex, there would be no people, no Buddha, no prophets, no Jesus. For example, there is nothing wrong with desiring food when you are hungry, and enjoying it as you eat. However, if we cling to that pleasure afterward, and then cling to the food that brought us pleasure, we start down the road to suffering. "That ice cream was so delicious, I need another big bowl." Or, upping the ante, "I worked so hard, I deserve another bowl."

Watching how often desire arises during the day brings it out of the unconscious realm, where it can control us, directing our behavior without our realizing it. "I want/need/deserve some ice cream" soon becomes "How did I gain ten pounds?" "I'm lonely and I want/need/deserve someone to love me" becomes "How did I find myself in bed with this person?" When desire is brought out into the open ground of our awareness, we can see it and make conscious decisions about whether following it would be wholesome or not.

Part of the reason desire is so potent is that it makes us feel alive. When our mind fixes on something it wants, we are like hunters fixed on our prey, alert and energized. If we are thinking of buying a car, we begin to notice cars everywhere. We talk to friends and salespeople about cars and read comparisons on the web. Finally we buy a car. We are happy driving our new car around. But how long does the pleasure last? A few weeks or months at most. Then it becomes just another car and we're off looking for something else, a new computer perhaps. Desire itself can be pleasurable, and desire satisfied can be disappointing, which is one reason people are always on the hunt, whether for a new car, a new partner, or a new taste treat. This very restlessness is the source of great suffering and dissatisfaction.

---

**Final Words:** When you are unhappy, discover what you are clinging to and let it go.

---

## 26

# Study Suffering

---

**The Exercise:** As you go about your day, pay attention to the phenomenon of suffering. How do you detect it in yourself or in others? Where is it most obvious? What are the milder forms? What are the more intense forms?

---

REMINDING YOURSELF

Post notes that say "Study Suffering," or photos of an unhappy person, in appropriate places.

DISCOVERIES

Suffering is everywhere. We see it in people's anxious faces, hear it in their voices, see it on the news. As we study suffering, we can hear it in our own thoughts, feel it in our own bodies, see it in the face in the mirror. Often people begin this exercise thinking of suffering in its extreme and obvious forms, the death of someone you love, or children who are victims of war. As this task brings increased awareness, people discover that there is a spectrum of suffering, from mild irritation and impatience to rage or overwhelming grief.

We are exposed to the suffering not just of people but of animals as well. We see the suffering of those we love and also the suffering of strangers on the street. Suffering pours into our hearts and minds through the radio, TV, and Internet.

There is a difference between pain and suffering. Pain is the unpleasant physical sensations experienced by all human bodies, indeed all sentient beings. Suffering is the mental and emotional distress that is added to these physical sensations. The Buddha studied suffering meticulously for seven years and discovered that physical pain is inevitable, but the suffering added by the mind is optional. Actually, it is only optional if you have good tools to work with the mind and if you apply them diligently.

For example, when we have a headache, we can think, "OK, I have temporary discomfort in this area of the body." Or we can think,

"This is the second headache I've had this week."
[Dragging the past into the present.]
"I'm sure it's going to get worse, like it did before."
[Predicting and perhaps creating future events.]
"I can't stand it." [But, in actuality, you have before and you will again.]
"What's wrong with me?" [Nothing. You are a human being with a body.]
"Could I have a brain tumor?" [Extremely unlikely, but you can give yourself a much worse headache worrying about it.]

"Maybe it's the stress I'm under at work. My boss is impossible . . . ." [Coasting around for someone to blame.]

Does our mental distress help cure the physical pain? No, it only makes it stronger and prolongs it. We have taken simple temporary physical discomfort and turned it into a mass of suffering.

## DEEPER LESSONS

There are some benefits to suffering. If we never experienced suffering, we would coast along in life with no motivation to change. Unfortunately it seems to be true that we are the most motivated to change when we are the most unhappy.

If we can restrain the mind from running amok, speculating and disaster-mongering, looking for someone to blame for our misery, then we can just experience the physical aspects of what we call "pain." If we just experience it, actually investigate it, discerning all its qualities, instead of it being "unbearable," it can become quite interesting. What size is the focus of pain? Exactly where is it located—above or below the skull? What is its texture—sharp, dull, prickly, or smooth? If it had a color, what would it be? Is it constant or intermittent? People often report interesting discoveries when they stop resisting pain and investigate it in this way. Resistance locks pain in. When we are not adding mental and emotional stress to simple physical discomfort, the pain is free to change and even to dissolve.

Suffering also gives birth to compassion in our hearts. After my first child was born, a new awareness of the fragility of life was also born, and I cried for all the unknown women around the world whose children had died. When we are in pain or in distress, it is a perfect time to change the direction of our awareness from inward to outward, and to do loving-kindness practice for all who suffer the same way that we are suffering right now. For example, when we are sick with the flu, we could say, "May all those who are sick in bed today, including me, be at ease. May we all rest well and recover quickly."

In the same way that being sick helps us appreciate good health, as we become aware of many kinds of suffering, we also become more aware of its opposite, the many simple sources of happiness—the perfect eyelashes of a baby, the smell of the first drops of rain on a dusty road, the slanting shafts of sunlight in a quiet room.

---

**Final Words:** Suffering gives us the motivation to change. Whether that change is positive or negative is up to us. Suffering also gives us the gift of empathy for all who suffer as we do.

---

## 27

# Silly Walking

---

**The Exercise:** Several times a day, especially when your state of mind is not optimal, do a silly walk of some kind. The easiest kinds of silly walking are these: walking backward, skipping, or hopping on one foot.

Watch what happens to your state of mind or mood as you walk in a silly way.

---

REMINDING YOURSELF

Put a small piece of tape on the tip of your shoe.

When you notice it, assess your mood, giving it a rating of 1 to 10 (with 1 being "miserable" and 10 being "very happy"). Then do a brief silly walk and assess your mood again. Any changes?

If you need inspiration, search on YouTube or other Internet video sites for the Monty Python sketch called "The Ministry of Silly Walks."

## DISCOVERIES

This task was inspired by Monty Python's "Ministry of Silly Walks." After watching this episode we were fooling around, inventing new ways to silly-walk. We discovered that silly walking is one of the fastest ways to change your mood, and the mood of those who are watching you. See if your kids will try it when they're being cranky!

The ability to change mind-states that are diving toward negative or depressed is a vital skill. Until we are adept at changing mind-states using the mind, we often have to recruit help from the body. Silly walking works because, as we say in Zen, the body and mind are not two. They are not separate or independent of each other.

## DEEPER LESSONS

We cannot depend upon people or things outside us to change our difficult emotions. Why not? First, because another person can never truly experience or know the state of our heart. In addition, people are what the Buddha called "conditioned things." This means that they are temporary, they will change, disappear, or die. At the very least they can't be available all the time, such as when we panic during a test or are distressed after a difficult job interview.

The Buddha advised his followers, "Be a lamp unto yourselves." This means that we can learn to turn on the bright light of our awakened mind and use it to look objectively at what is happening in the machinery of self. By means of this clear light we can observe when and how the small self is not functioning optimally, and we can learn how to fix it.

When we learn to change an unwholesome mood by ourselves, rather than being the victim of our changing emotions and thoughts, we are becoming what is called in Zen the "Master or Mistress of the House." Through diligent practice we can become confident about our ability to change our thoughts and moods as required by each situation. Then our fear of being a human being living in the midst of constant and unpredictable change begins to dissipate. We can experience a taste of true liberation—liberation from the tyranny of our mind and its fluctuating emotions.

Doing this task we are reminded to take ourselves lightly. Silly walking moves our mind from its preoccupation with ourselves and our predicaments and changes our perspective. The Japanese Buddhist master Shonin said that we humans are "foolish and ignorant beings." When we acknowledge our own foolishness, when we are willing even to *be* foolish, many possibilities open up.

---

**Final Words:** We can learn to change our unwholesome moods and thoughts by ourselves, without any equipment or expense. Like any skill, it takes time and lots of practice.

---

## 28

# Water

---

The Exercise: Open your awareness to water, in all its forms, both inside and outside of your body and dwelling. Become aware of liquidity, in food, drinks, and in your environment.

---

REMINDING YOURSELF

Post the word "Water" or images of water drops. You can also place small bowls of water in strategic places.

DISCOVERIES

Doing this exercise, we realize that water is everywhere. It is inside us, in saliva, tears, blood, urine, gastric juices, joint fluid, and sexual secretions. We are 70 percent water; without it we would be a small pile of dry cells and salts. Without it we would be dead in a few days. We take water in all day long, in tea and tangerines, in salad greens and soup. It is outside us, in puddles, damp soil, leaves, dew, and windshield wiper fluid. It is above us in clouds. It runs beneath us in the earth in sewers, water pipes, and deep aquifers.

When we open our awareness to water, we realize what a miraculous substance it is. It is transparent but can take on infinite colors. It conforms to any vessel. It is an invisible gas we breathe in and out without even noticing, a transparent fluid we pour down our throats with gratitude, white crystal flakes that cover the ugliness humans can create, or a slippery solid that makes us fearful of walking or driving.

Ordinarily we don't pay attention to water unless there's a problem with it—the water is shut off, the toilet overflows, or the road to work is flooded. In developed countries we take clean water for granted. The Buddha, who lived in a hot, unsanitary country 2,550 years ago, spoke of clean water for washing and drinking as one of the greatest of gifts. There is growing concern that our world supply of water will run out. There are still many people in the world without safe drinking water. Can we appreciate this life-sustaining gift, given each day by earth and sky?

A young monk once heated water from the river for his master's bath. When he tipped a few drops of water left in his wooden bucket out onto the ground, his master scolded him vigorously for his lack of mindfulness. Even a single drop of water could be given to a plant in the garden, thus giving life to the plant, to the monks, to the dharma, or back to the river itself. The monk's mind was opened. He took the name

Tekisui, meaning "one drop," and went on to become a great master.

As we become mindful of water, our mind can take on its flowing quality. Just as water is able to flow without hindrance into different containers, when we cultivate a light, flexible mind, we are able to flow into situations as they arise and change, without energy-sapping resistance.

We enjoy sitting by a river or stream, watching the endlessly changing, constant flow. Can we watch the flow of our life with calm eyes as well, at ease with impermanence, with the endless flow of cause and effect?

When we observe how water moves between its different forms, from solid to liquid to gas, we also learn something about our lives and the truth of impermanence. A collection of elements condenses temporarily into an apparently solid human being, but when the forces holding these elements in balance change (a drop in blood potassium, an irregular heartbeat, a moment's inattention at the wheel), they begin to separate and dissolve, and are released back into hydrogen, carbon, calcium, oxygen, and a bit of heat.

Water has another quality we can learn from. When muddy water is poured into a glass and allowed to sit undisturbed, eventually the mud settles to the bottom and the water becomes clear again. When our mind is agitated, anxious, or fearful, it is hard to see any solutions to our problems. One aspect of mindfulness is remembering that it is possible to still the mind and let it regain its natural clarity. Just sit down, take a few deep breaths, and allow your thoughts and feelings to settle. How? By doing one of the practices in this book. The most potent techniques to use in an urgent situation are the following: becoming aware of your breath, becoming aware of your *hara*, doing loving-kindness for your body and mind, and opening your ears to sounds. It's refreshing, like giving your mind a bath.

**Final Words:** Zen Master Dogen instructed his cooks, "See water as your lifeblood."

# 29

# Look Up!

**The Exercise:** Several times a day, deliberately look up. Take a few minutes to really look at the ceiling in rooms, at tall buildings, at the tops of trees, at roofs, at hills or mountains, and at the sky. See what new things you notice.

REMINDING YOURSELF

Post little signs with upward-pointing arrows or the words "Look Up."

DISCOVERIES

Most of the time we only look at a narrow wedge of the world. Because our eyes are in front of our head, our visual awareness is usually limited to what is in front of us, a slice from the ground up to about ten feet. Only when we see or hear something unusual, such as a seven-foot-tall man or a sudden loud noise above us, do we look up. Of course people in some occupations, such as farmers or sailors, often scan the sky since incoming weather is important to them, but these days they may be more likely to look at a weather channel or a radar screen.

Looking up opens our perspective, letting the mind out of its neurotic squirrel cage and allowing it to stretch and flex. When looking up, people notice many things they hadn't seen before: light fixtures on ceilings, decorative carvings on buildings, treetops tossing in the wind, the shapes and colors of clouds, people looking out of apartment windows or leaning over balconies, birds suddenly wheeling in tight formation.

There are psychological experiments that show how much we miss seeing, even when we are looking directly at something. For example, people don't notice when someone in a gorilla suit strolls through a basketball game, when faces are switched in a photo of two people, or when a person they are asking directions of is exchanged for another person (when hidden briefly from view by a man walking by carrying a board). We walk around caught up in a dream and three-quarters blind.

DEEPER LESSONS

"Looking" is not equivalent to actually seeing. To see something requires not only vision, but attention. The gorilla in the basketball game is not seen because we have been asked to focus on something else, to count the number of passes one team makes. We can drive to work, with our eyes apparently seeing stoplights, but without any conscious awareness of whether we stopped or not.

We are so preoccupied with the things right in front of us that we miss much of what goes on all around us. Children are more aware than adults, whose anxiety has narrowed their lives to "What do I have to worry is coming toward me?" Looking up expands the size of our life to include many more beings (such as birds) and phenomena (such as rainbows) than before. When our vista is wider, our experience of self expands, too. We aren't so trapped in the small box we call "me, my world, and my worries."

Looking up helps us broaden our perspective. How does the lady on the fifth-story balcony or the eagle circling overhead see us? When we can see even a little bit through their eyes, through God's eyes, the claustrophobic closet of our self-obsessed life opens and we get a tantalizing taste of freedom. Looking up is looking out—out of the small box called "my self." Won't you step out?

---

**Final Words:** The eyes are an important tool of mindfulness. Open up your field of vision and really look!

---

## 30

# Defining and Defending

The Exercise: Become aware of how you define yourself and defend yourself and your personal territory. For example, do you see yourself as a Liberal or a Conservative? An East Coast person or West Coast person? How do you defend that position? Notice how quickly a mug, parking place, or seat on the subway becomes "mine," and how you react when someone else takes it.

Check in on this process several times a day. In particular when you get irritated or upset, ask, "How am I defining myself or my personal territory at this moment?"

REMINDING YOURSELF

Post notes that say "Defining and Defending?" in appropriate spots.

DISCOVERIES

This practice originated with a teacher in the Tibetan Buddhist lineage named Michael Conklin. He teaches a course on Buddhism at a community college near our monastery. One of the assignments he gives his students is to spend a week watching the process of "defining and defending the self." The students find it quite revealing. Their major discovery is that they are engaged in this process continually.

We can see this process clearly when we define a particular physical space as belonging to us, a chair or desk in a classroom, a corner table in a favorite restaurant, a space on the highway, a shelf in a closet, or a spot on the floor in an exercise class. If someone doesn't respect the invisible boundaries around the territory we have staked out in our mind, we react. Within minutes of putting down our yoga mat, we have declared the space "mine." At our monastery we have to be careful about moving anyone's meditation cushions once a retreat begins, because it can really upset some folks. We tend to make little safe nests wherever we go and then we defend them.

This process starts early in life. Zen teacher Shohaku Okamura tells how he took his young son to a park. He brought along several toys so that his son could share them with other kids and get to know some American children. But as the other kids approached, his son gathered the toys to his breast and uttered his first English words, "No, mine!" Thus a self is born and defended. It is a natural process in human development, but for us to be truly content, it has to be modified in adult life.

Greed arises when we think we need something in order to complete ourselves and to be happy. It could be a certain car, house, food, an academic degree, or public acclaim. It could be another person. If we can't have what we have set our heart on, we become unhappy. This is defining ourselves by material possessions, that which we can manage to get and hold on to.

We also define ourselves by our mental possessions, showing off our knowledge and vigorously defending our points of view. We think, "My opinions about this topic are the correct ones and I'll argue until I convince you!" This is astounding and amusing, when you consider that in a group of twenty-four people there are twenty-three different opinions besides our own. Why would we think ours is the only one that is correct?

Anger or irritation is a clue that we are defending the self. Anger arises when we think we need to get rid of something or someone in order to be happy. It could be a certain politician, a pain or illness, a disagreeable boss or coworker, a pesky neighbor or his barking dog. If we can't get rid of them, we become unhappy. Why won't the world cooperate with what I want to happen? Again, this is astounding and amusing. Why won't things go my way and not the way desired by the other seven billion people on the planet?

We are also ignorant about what our self is. It is not one steady, stable thing. It is always in flux. Everything we call "me" is an ever-changing process that affects our likes and dislikes, our clothes, hair, and every cell in our body. Each breath is part of that constant flow. When we try to freeze our sense of self, we only create suffering. ("I feel thirty years old on the inside, but I look sixty on the outside and I hate it!")

---

**Final Words:** There is no thing called a self to defend, because in reality the self is a process of constantly changing sensations, including the sensations we call thoughts.

---

## 31

# Notice Smells

The Exercise: During this week, as often as possible, become aware of smells and fragrance. This may be easiest to do when you are eating or drinking, but try it at other times, too. Several times a day, try sniffing the air like a dog. If there are not many smells in your environment, you might try creating some smells that you can detect. You could dab some vanilla on your wrist, or boil some spices, such as cinnamon or cloves, in water on the stove. You could also try lighting a few scented candles or sniffing scented oils.

REMINDING YOURSELF
Post the word "Smell" or an image of a nose in helpful places.

DISCOVERIES
The cells that respond to smells in the back of our nose are just two synapses away from the processing centers in our

primitive brain for emotion and memories, so odors can evoke powerful conditioned responses—desire and aversion. These unconscious responses can occur even when we are not aware of detecting an odor. We don't appreciate our sense of smell until we lose it, for example, when we have a cold. People who lose their sense of smell permanently can become depressed, since they also lose their previous enjoyment of food. Many become anxious that they will not smell smoke from a fire, will fail to detect their own body odor, or will eat spoiled food.

When practicing mindfulness of smell people discover that there are many smells in their environment, some obvious (coffee, cinnamon rolls, gasoline, skunk) and many that are more subtle (fresh air as we step outside, soap or shaving cream on our own face, clean sheets). They also discover that smell can evoke emotion, desire and aversion.

The rich experience of what we call flavor is mostly due to our sense of smell. Our tongue is only able to register a few sensations—salty, sweet, sour, bitter, and umami (savory, such as in meat or soy sauce)—but we can distinguish several thousand odors and as little as one molecule of some substances. Research shows that women have more sensitive noses than men. Women may wear perfume to attract men, but the effort is probably wasted. The fragrances men pick as favorites are the smell of baking bread, vanilla, and grilling meat.

In reality, there are no "good" or "bad" smells. We become accustomed to common smells around us. When I lived in Africa, people around me had a strong aroma of sweat mixed with wood smoke. It was undoubtedly a comforting smell to a child who had been surrounded by that fragrance since birth. Probably I smelled funny to them, and they could also detect me coming in the dark.

When East and West first met, Japanese people, who bathed daily, disliked the smell of Europeans, who ate dairy products and took baths infrequently. They called the visitors "stinks of butter." One is not very aware of the odor of one's own body. Other people may tell us, to our surprise, that we need to take a shower or that we have a delicious smell. Just as we are not aware of the scent of our own body, we are not aware of the "scent" of our own personality. How does that affect others?

## DEEPER LESSONS

Much of our behavior is directed by unconscious conditioning. We meet a person who looks, dresses, speaks, or even smells like someone who wounded us in our childhood, and we feel an instant, inexplicable aversion toward this innocent person. It has nothing to do with them. It is just an electrical phenomenon, sense impressions causing neurons to fire and connect to storage sites in the brain for old memories and emotions. To transform these habitual patterns is not easy. First we have to bring the light of awareness to the body sensations, thoughts, and emotions as they arise. We have to watch carefully the junction between sensation and feeling tone, which is the seed crystal that will start a chain reaction that ends in thought, emotion, speech, and behavior (or what Buddhists call karma).

The cascade of *sensation* —> *feeling* (*tone*) —> *perception* —> *action* happens so fast that it is hard to see the individual steps. But people can understand this chain of events when it involves smell. Let's say you step outside and take a deep breath. You detect a smell and recoil internally. Why? As chemical molecules hit the inside of your nose, you smelled something, and it caused a negative feeling tone, before your mind knew what it was. Then your mind tried to identify it—"Oh, dog feces." This is perception, which is then followed by volitional action. You might say, "What idiot let their dog poop on my lawn?!" Or you might just walk inside to get a plastic bag to clean it up.

Odor can have a powerful effect on our mental-emotional state and behavior. Smells can call up memories and old reactions. For example, the smell of a certain aftershave your father used could make you either happy and affectionate or irritable and standoffish, depending upon how you and your dad got along. Psychologists sometimes use disgusting smells to decondition destructive impulses or behaviors, such as addiction to pornography.

Positive conditioning to smell can be helpful. One reason incense is used in meditation halls is that over time a strong link is forged between the fragrance of incense and a quiet concentrated state of mind. As you enter the scented hall, your mind automatically settles. Monks become so sensitive to smell during long hours of meditation that they can tell when the meditation period is over by the smell of the incense. It changes when the burning tip reaches the bed of ash in the incense bowl.

We can be very alert to fragrance when our mind is quiet and input to the other senses is minimal. One night I was sitting outdoors at a temple in Japan, in the deep dark of the monastery's forest of giant bamboo. It was the seventh day of a silent retreat. The air was fresh after two days of typhoon rain. My mind was completely still and my awareness open wide. In the silence I could hear a single bamboo leaf softly falling, down, down. Gradually I became aware of a subtle spicy fragrance. It came from the bamboo. I have never been able to smell it since.

I will always remember its delicate perfume, and that remembering evokes in me the sublime peace of that night.

---

**Final Words:** One of the most subtly pleasurable meditations is to be fully aware of smell, how it changes with each in-breath and out-breath.

---

## 32

# This Person Could Die Tonight

---

**The Exercise:** Several times a day, when someone is talking to you, in person or on the telephone, remind yourself, "This person could die tonight. This may be the last time I will be with them." Notice any changes in how you listen, speak, or interact with them.

---

REMINDING YOURSELF

Put a note on your bathroom mirror, just above or below where your own reflection appears, saying, "This Person Could Die Tonight." Put similar notes near your telephone or in your workspace—places where you're likely to see them while you're interacting with others.

DISCOVERIES

Some people find this exercise a bit depressing at first, but they soon discover that when they become aware of their own mortality and that of the person they are talking to, they listen and pay attention in a different way. Their heart opens as they hold the truth that this could be the very last time they will see this person alive. When we talk to people, especially people we see daily, we are easily distracted and only half listen. We often look a bit to the side or down at something else, rather than directly at them. We might even be annoyed that they have interrupted us. It takes the realization that they could die to make us look at them anew.

This practice becomes particularly poignant when the person you are talking to is aged or ill, or when death has recently taken an acquaintance or someone you loved. When the Japanese say good-bye to someone, they stand respectfully, watching and waving until the car or train is out of sight. This custom has its origin in the awareness that this could be the last time they will see one another. How sad we would feel if our last encounter with our child, partner, or parent were flavored with impatience or anger! How comforting if we had said good-bye with care.

DEEPER LESSONS

Although sickness, old age, and death come to everyone who has been born into this world, we carry out our lives as if this will not be true for us or those we care about. This practice helps us break through our denial that human life is quite fragile and that death could come at any moment. All it takes is a slight change in the potassium level in our blood, a virulent bacteria, an oncoming driver who falls asleep, or an odd electrical pattern in our heart. Occasionally the veil of denial lifts and we see the truth of the fragility of human life, such as when a coworker or a family member is diagnosed with a fatal illness or when someone our age or younger dies unexpectedly.

Of course we do not want to fill our mind with constant, anxious thoughts about mortality, but an awareness of impermanence can help us cherish the people we encounter every day. When the veil is parted, and we experience the truth that every human life is brief, our conversations change. Instead of talking "to" someone, with a mind half full of other thoughts, we bring more presence to each encounter. This quiet attentiveness is an unusual occurrence in the world of ordinary human beings.

We fall asleep each night in complete trust that we will awaken. When we realize that we, too, could die tonight, we can become more present, more alive within each moment of our life.

At our Zen monastery, we have a chant that is sung at the end of each day of a silent retreat. You may wish to recite it each night for a week before you go to sleep:

May I respectfully remind you,
Life and death are of supreme importance.
Time swiftly passes by and opportunity is lost.
When this day has passed, our days of life will be
    decreased by one.
Each of us should strive to awaken.
*Awaken!*
*Take heed!*
Do not squander your life!

---

**Final Words:** Becoming aware of death opens our awareness to this single, vivid moment of life.

---

## 33

# Hot and Cold

---

The Exercise: Pay attention during this week to the sensations of heat and cold. Notice any physical or emotional reaction to temperature or temperature changes. Practice being at ease no matter what the temperature is.

---

REMINDING YOURSELF

You can put up little signs with an image of a thermometer, or with the words "Hot and Cold."

DISCOVERIES

Doing this exercise, we watch our aversion to temperatures outside of a small range. Each person's range is different. We complain, "It's too hot!" or "It's too cold!" as if it shouldn't be that way—the sun, clouds, and air have conspired to make us uncomfortable. We're always doing something to adjust the temperature, turning heaters and air conditioners on and off, opening and closing windows and doors, donning and shedding clothing. We're never satisfied for long. When the temperature rises above 90 degrees, we long for cooler weather; during the cold, rainy winters, we long for sun.

I can remember childhood summers in Missouri. The vinyl upholstery in the car scalded our legs as we got in and there were pools of sweat under us as we got out. We played outside, got sticky, sweaty, and never complained. It was just the way it was. Parents of young children often remark that when they go to the beach, their kids will get in the water and have a ball no matter what the temperature of the ocean. What happens as we mature that makes us intolerant of the way things are?

Once, we were on peace pilgrimage in Japan in August, where stepping out the door felt like we were entering a sauna. Within a few minutes our clothes were soaked through with sweat. After a few hours salt encrusted our skin and made white rings on our clothes. It was so hard not to give vent to our discomfort. But we noticed that the Japanese people, from babies to very old people, were just going about their business, apparently unaffected. It inspired us to let go of complaining-mind and just be present with things as they were, sensations as merely sensations, the wet and dry places, the hot exterior and cool interior, the tickling of trickling sweat. The suffering inflicted by the mind lifted and we became much happier pilgrims.

A woman came to me during a retreat saying that despite extra layers of clothing and a hot-water bottle, she felt cold all the time. She also realized that she was frightened about feeling cold. She knew the fear was irrational, and she had been looking for its source. Then she remembered an incident twenty years earlier when she'd had some heart trouble and was very cold.

I asked her to scan her body carefully and tell me what percentage of the body did not feel cold. After a few minutes she reported with surprise that over 90 percent of her body felt warm, or even hot. She realized that the 10 percent of her body that was cool was producing 100 percent of the fear. Later she said that a weight had been lifted from her mind, a fear that had lasted decades, and she was now able easily to tolerate different temperatures.

I once watched a passenger get into my car and reach over to turn on the air conditioner, before the car had even started. It's like salting our food before we taste it. We live on automatic, trying to insulate ourselves against any discomfort before it even arrives. Then we lose the joy of potential discovery and the freedom of finding that we can investigate, and even be happy, within a greater range of experiences than we thought.

DEEPER LESSONS

A very important way to work with discomfort is to stop avoiding it. You walk right into it, and feel from within the body what is true. You investigate the discomfort, its size, shape, surface texture, and even its color or sound. Is it constant or intermittent? When you are this attentive, when your meditative absorption is deep, what we call discomfort or pain begins to shift and even disappear. It becomes a series of sensations just appearing and disappearing in empty space, twinkling on and off. It is most interesting.

In Japan the *zendo,* or meditation hall, is not heated in winter. The windows are open. It is just like sitting outside except that you don't get rained or snowed on—much. During one

February-long retreat I put on every bit of clothing in my suitcase, so many layers I could barely bend my knees to sit. My skin was so icy it was painful to let my attention rest on my exposed face or hands even briefly. During traditional Zen retreats you eat your meals in the zendo. While eating I had to look to see if the chopsticks were still wedged in my numb fingers. There was no way out of this discomfort. The only way to go was in, placing an unwavering concentration deep in my belly, in the *hara*, or center of the body. It was a powerful retreat and I understood why the revered Zen master Sogaku Harada Roshi insisted that his monastery be built deep in the snow country.

We spend so much effort trying to make external conditions suit us. However, it is impossible for us to remain comfortable all the time, for the nature of all things is change. This attempt at control is at the heart of our physical exhaustion and emotional distress. There is a Zen koan about this. A monk asked Master Tozan, "Cold and heat descend upon us. How can we avoid them?" Tozan replied, "Why don't you go to the place where there is no cold or heat?" The monk was puzzled and asked, "Where is the place where there is no cold or heat?" Tozan said, "When it is cold, let it be so cold that it kills you. When hot, let it be so hot that it kills you."

In this teaching, "kill you" means kill your ideas about how things have to be for you to be happy. It may sound odd, but you can be practicing mindfulness with discomfort or pain and be quite happy. This happiness comes from the pleasure of just being present, and also from the confidence that you are gaining—confidence that, with ongoing practice, you will eventually be able to face whatever life brings you, even pain, aided by tools such as mindfulness.

**Final Words:** When your mind says "too hot" or "too cold," don't believe it. Investigate the entire body's experience of heat and cold.

## 34

# The Great Earth beneath You

---

The Exercise: As often as possible, become aware of the great earth beneath you. Become aware through sight and touch, especially the touches on the bottoms of the feet. When you are not outside, you can use your imagination to "feel" the earth beneath the floor you are on or the building you are in.

---

REMINDING YOURSELF

Place notes with the word "Earth" or pictures of the globe in appropriate places in your environment. You could also put some dirt in a small dish on your desk, countertop, or dining room table.

DISCOVERIES

At the monastery we decided to begin this mindfulness practice each day by touching our forehead to the floor as soon as we got out of bed. It seemed like an odd practice at first, but we all came to appreciate it. Although we do many full bows each day as part of our Zen practice (touching our heads to the floor of the meditation hall), this morning practice had a feeling of poignant vulnerability that we did not experience in our other daily bows. To wake up, stand, and immediately kneel and touch the forehead to the ground helped us begin the day with humility and with gratitude for the earth that holds us to itself. We ended the day with the same bow before bed, an acknowledgment and expression of gratitude to the ever-supportive earth.

All day long we humans are walking and driving around on the surface of the earth and we are almost completely unaware of the huge ball that is our platform for life. We are equally unaware of the force of gravity that the earth exerts on us. Becoming aware of the earth beneath us—supporting our every step, grounding our lives—is deeply encouraging for many people.

When we are "up in our heads," distracted and ruminating, we are easily pushed off balance. If our attention is extended through the bottoms of our feet into the earth, we feel rooted, more solid and less swayed by thoughts and emotions or unexpected events.

The Zen monk Thich Nhat Hanh writes,

> I like to walk alone on country paths, rice plants and wild grasses on both sides, putting each foot down on the earth in mindfulness, knowing that I walk on the wondrous earth. In such moments, existence is a miraculous and mysterious reality. People usually consider walking on water or in thin air a miracle. But I think the real miracle is to walk on earth . . . a miracle we don't even recognize.

## DEEPER LESSONS

The Buddha gave the following instructions to his son, Rahula,

Develop meditation that is like the earth: as the earth is not troubled by agreeable or disagreeable things it comes into contact with, so if you meditate like the earth, agreeable and disagreeable experiences will not trouble you.

The Buddha observed that you can pour any liquid, pleasant rose water or unpleasant sewage, onto the earth, and the earth remains solid and immovable. The earth keeps supporting us no matter what we humans create—beauty or war. Whatever's happening on the surface of our planet, the earth lies firmly beneath us. Mindfulness, meditation, or prayer has the power to train our heart and mind to rest in a state that is equally steady and untroubled.

Of course, recognizing the stable, immovable quality of the earth does not mean we should be unconcerned about the health of our planet and allow it to be polluted. However, it is also very important that we not let our worry for the environment poison our mind. Once, my Zen teacher Maezumi Roshi attended an international conference on environmental awareness in Buenos Aires, Argentina. He had never shown much interest in environmental issues and we (his students) were pleased that this conference might educate him. When he returned, we asked him what he had learned. He told us that the conference was held in a group of university buildings that were arranged around a green commons area. He had spent the week watching how environmental activists took shortcuts across the grass instead of walking on the paths, eventually turning the little park into a sea of mud. To him, this was a living example of the ignorance at the root of all human problems. Everyone was ignoring the grass and earth as they talked and fretted about how to make humankind care for the earth.

We can think and talk a lot about a problem, but if that prevents us from being present or from developing an unpolluted mind, the problem we're seeking to address will remain unsolved.

---

**Final Words:** If I could maintain constant awareness of the entire earth beneath my feet and also awareness of myself as a tiny, temporary, animated speck crawling about on its surface, I might need no other practice.

---

## 35

# Notice Dislike

The Exercise: Become aware of aversion, the arising of negative feelings toward something or someone. These could be mild feelings, such as irritation, or strong feelings, such as anger and hatred. Try to see what happened just before the aversion arose. What sense impressions occurred— sight, sound, touch, taste, smell, or thought? When does aversion first arise during the day?

### REMINDING YOURSELF

Post the words "Notice Dislike" in places where aversion might arise, such as on your mirror, TV, computer monitor, and car dashboard. You could also use small pictures of someone frowning.

### DISCOVERIES

When we do this exercise, we find that aversion is more common in our mental/emotional landscape than we realized. It may begin our day, arising when the alarm rings, or as we get out of bed and find that our back hurts. It can be triggered by events on the morning news, by a long line at the subway or gas station, or by an encounter with family, coworkers, or clients.

Once, I was waiting in the car for my husband to come out of the house. I looked idly out the window and noticed that near the fence many long dandelions had grown up and they were going to seed. Instantaneously an impulse arose to jump out of the car, grab some pruning shears, and whack them back into submission. This was accompanied by the thought, "Off with their heads!" I realized that this was the seed of anger, the seed of all the wars waged on this earth, lying dormant within me. It's not that I hate dandelions. Their bright golden faces are a wonderful thing to meditate upon. Close up, they can change a negative mind-state quite quickly. It's not that I intend to let them flourish, but if I trim that part of the lawn, I will wait until I am not doing it from aversion. I might ride the mower practicing appreciation for the life of the dandelions and loving-kindness for all the beings who make their home in the grass and weeds.

DEEPER LESSONS

It may be dismaying to discover how pervasive aversion is in even a single day in a life that we might describe as happy. It is, however, very important to become aware that feelings of dislike are ubiquitous in our daily lives. Aversion is one of the three afflictive mind-states described in the Buddhist tradition—greed (or clinging), aversion (or pushing away), and delusion (or ignoring). They are called afflictive because they afflict us the way a virus afflicts us, causing distress and pain not only to ourselves but to those around us.

Aversion is the hidden source of anger and aggression. It arises from the notion that if we could just manage to get rid of something or someone, then we would be happy. What we humans wish to get rid of in order to become happy could be as trivial as a mosquito or as large as a nation.

There are few ideas more absurd than the notion, "If I could arrange things—and people—to be just as I want them, then I would be happy." It is absurd for at least two reasons. First of all, even if we had the power to make everything in the world perfect for us, that perfection could only last a second because all the other people in the world have different ideas of how they would like things to be and are working to get them their way. Our "perfect" is not perfect to anyone else. Secondly, forcing perfection on the world is bound to fail because of the truth of impermanence—nothing lasts forever.

Sometimes as I am walking around the monastery, I notice a subtle flavor in my mind. It is a faint but pervasive sense of aversion. It comes from what I consider to be part of my job, noticing things that need to be fixed or changed. It comes from noticing imperfection. When this necessary noticing makes my mind-state go sour, I have to switch for a while to "appreciating things as they are."

Mindfulness practice helps us to become at ease no matter what conditions exist, and no matter how they change. It asks us to see the perfection in all creation. It asks us to become aware of aversion and counteract it with appreciation and loving-kindness.

**Final Words:** One of the Buddha's famous sayings is, "Anger does not cease through anger, but through love alone." Become aware of aversion within and use the antidote—practice loving-kindness.

# 36

# Are You Overlooking Something?

**The Exercise:** Several times a day, pause to notice what you're paying attention to at that moment and then open your senses to see if you can discover what you've been failing to notice. Our attention is usually selective. What are you ignoring?

## REMINDING YOURSELF

Post notes around your environment that ask, "Ignoring?" (Don't ignore the notes!) You might also set an alarm to help you stop several times a day to do this practice.

## DISCOVERIES

We go about our days with a narrow focus. We attend to the sound of the alarm clock, what our mind says is on our to do list for the day, what's on the TV or computer screen, the voice on our cell phone. Our attention widens only when something unusual occurs. A loud bang! The ears are alert. Is that a car backfiring or was it a gunshot? Or the weather suddenly changes and we look up at the sky for the first time in weeks, or maybe months.

When we stop and purposely enlarge our sphere of listening and seeing, we realize that there is so much happening that we are missing. We've been blocking out the sounds of the refrigerator humming, the sounds of traffic, the feel of the ground under our feet, the position of the sun in the sky, the many colors in the linoleum on the floor. We may notice that when we enlarge the realm of our attention, there is a sense of relief and relaxation, as if it took a great deal of energy to hold a narrow focus.

It's impossible for us to pay full attention to two things at once (unless our mind is exceptionally well trained). Try it. Pay full attention to the bottoms of your feet, feeling every sensation of warmth, tingling, pressure. Notice where the sensations are the strongest and where they might be absent. Now try to hold that awareness while quietly counting backward by sevens from one hundred. You can feel the mind trying to hold two things at once, flickering back and forth between the feet and the mental math.

If our mind isn't made to be fully attentive to two things at once, then we are always ignoring a lot of things. For example, most of the time we ignore our breathing, letting our body breathe by itself. When people first begin practicing mindfulness of the breath, bringing the mind's attention to the simple act of breathing, they can tie themselves in knots trying to figure out what a "normal" breath is. How long or deep should it be? Should they move only their chest or also their belly? They have to learn not to interfere with the breath or force it, to let

their mind witness the breath as if they are watching themselves breathe at night when they are deeply asleep.

When we focus our attention on the breath, we cannot attend to our list of things to worry about. That is how breath
meditation can lower blood pressure and reduce stress.

### DEEPER LESSONS

Ignoring the countless sights, sensations, and sounds that im-
pinge on our eyes, skin, and ears may be essential when we
need to focus on getting tasks done, such as reading a book
before an exam, writing a sensitive e-mail, or getting a high
score on a video game, but all that sensory blocking takes energy. When we are able to let go of those invisible shields and
open our awareness to all that surrounds us, it is like stepping
out of a cramped, musty room and finding ourselves in a large
alpine meadow. Eye doctors tell us that if we are focused on a
nearby object such as a book or video screen for a long period
of time, we need to refresh our eyes (and protect our eyesight)
by looking at something in the distance at regular intervals.
The same advice applies to our mind. We need to let it out of its
tiny box regularly, letting it expand as far and wide as it is able.

When we pay attention to what we are paying attention
to, that is, when we watch what our mind is focused on, we
discover that our range of attention is normally quite limited.
Likewise, our worldview is self-centered. *Self-centered* is not a
pejorative term in Buddhism. Rather, it is simply a description
of how all humans naturally focus on themselves. Specifically,
most of our attention is devoted to pursuing what gives us
pleasure, avoiding what is potentially dangerous or unpleasant,
and ignoring everything else. I will pursue the beautiful girl,

avoid that homeless man, and ignore the person standing next to me in the checkout line.

When we sit in meditation, or enter contemplative prayer, we let go of the mind's schemes for pursuing or avoiding. We acknowledge how much we have been ignoring during our busy day. We deliberately open our awareness as wide as possible, encompassing all that is, just as it is, the movement of our ribs as we breathe, the humming of the ventilation system, the scent of perfume left by someone who has left the room, and the picture that arises in the mind of the candy bar lying in our desk drawer. We notice it all, without any internal dialogue, without any criticism or judgment. We notice that when internal dialogue does begin, our field of sensory awareness instantly shuts down. Then we quiet the inner voices and open our awareness once again.

In Zen this is called "not knowing." It is a special kind of ignorance, a very wise kind of ignorance. When we rest in not knowing, many possibilities open up. We may hear things we didn't know were there—a cricket chirping or the start of a gentle rain. We might even hear a quiet inner voice telling us some important truths.

---

**Final Words:** For a pause that refreshes, at least once a day, stop trying to know and do. Open your awareness and simply sit in "not knowing."

---

## 37

# The Wind

The Exercise: Become aware of the movement of air, both in obvious forms, such as wind, and in subtler forms, such as the breath.

Post the word "Wind" in helpful places at home and at work.

DISCOVERIES

Wind has many forms, from hard gales to soft breaths. If we bring this exercise to mind and open the senses several times a day for an entire week, we will begin to notice the more subtle ways air moves. People make wind. There is the movement of air in your breath, when you sniff, when you blow on a hot beverage, when you sigh. There is the touch of moving air on your body when you walk, even indoors. There is air moving in many appliances, such as clothes dryers, microwaves, and refrigerators.

One person noticed that his body perceives wind and creates goose bumps on his skin before his mind can register that a cool breeze is present. Our body is aware of our environment even when we aren't, when we have gone unconscious or are asleep. It moves to protect us by raising up our hair follicles to create an insulating layer next to the skin, like a thin down jacket. Some old masters pointed to this as an example of our inherent Buddha nature, which cares for us continually.

As our senses become more refined, we discover that whenever we move, we create air movement. Speaking is air movement. Any sound is air movement. A sailor explained to us that the wind is continuously circling the entire earth. When he's in his boat, he is acutely aware of the wind and the weather it will bring because not to be aware of this in the middle of the ocean could mean death. In gale winds his boat has to be kept directly facing the wind, or it can be overturned in a flash.

Learning to sail involves learning to "read" the wind by noticing small changes on the surface of the water or in the direction of a flag or telltale (a piece of cloth attached to the boat). If there are no flags or telltales visible, a sailor can determine the direction of the wind by observing shorebirds such as seagulls, who always stand facing directly into the wind so that their feathers won't be ruffled. This mindfulness exercise invites us to develop this kind of sensitivity to the changing winds.


DEEPER LESSONS

How do we know that wind exists? Take a moment and ponder this.

There are four ways we experience "wind": by feeling its touch, by feeling a change in temperature, by seeing it move other things, and by hearing it move through other things. What we call wind is essentially change, change in what we see (leaves moving), change in what we feel (cooler skin), or change in what we hear (a howling sound). We only know the existence of wind indirectly, through the nerve impulses that travel from our skin, tympanic membrane, and retinas. Actually, this is true of all that we perceive. We cannot know reality directly. There is no way to prove the independent existence of any other thing since our awareness of these others is created by electrical impulses in our nervous system.

When the mind is deeply quiet, then anything can bring sudden awakening, even the wind. In his youth Zen master Yamada Mumon was very sick with tuberculosis. Doctors predicted his death and gave up treating him. He lived in isolation for several years, resigned to death, and his mind gradually became serene and still. One bright, clear summer day he saw some flowers in the garden blown by the wind and was deeply awakened to the existence of a great power. He realized that this vast energy had given life to him and to all beings, embracing him and living through him. He wrote the following poem, and soon afterward his fatal illness was cured:

All things are embraced
Within the universal mind
Told by the cool wind
This morning.

What Mumon Roshi called "the universal mind" has been given many names. It has no boundaries. It reaches everywhere, throughout space and time. And yet, it does not manifest as anything other than each small thing, each breath, each sound, each falling flower petal floating on the wind.

---

**Final Words:** There is a subtle mindfulness practice of becoming aware of the breath at the nostrils. Try it. For hours. There is no risk, except the possibility of becoming more awake to the subtle changes that make up the fabric of our lives.

---

# Listen Like a Sponge

---

**The Exercise:** Listen to other people as if you were a sponge, soaking up whatever the other person says. Let the mind be quiet, and just take it in. Don't formulate any response in the mind until a response is requested or obviously needed.

---

### REMINDING YOURSELF

Post the words "Listen Like a Sponge," or a picture of an ear and a sponge, in relevant places.

### DISCOVERIES

At our monastery we call this practice absorptive listening, and we've discovered that it does not come naturally to most people. Some people, musicians for example, have been trained to listen with absorptive attention to musical sounds, but that does not mean they are able to listen in the same way when a person is talking to them. Good psychotherapists use absorptive listening. They are attuned to the subtle changes in tone or quality of voice that indicate something deeper than the words, even belying the words, a sticking place, hidden tears or anger, that needs to be explored.

Lawyers are trained to do the opposite, especially if they work in the adversarial atmosphere of the courtroom. They are listening for the flaws or discrepancies in what someone is saying, while simultaneously forming a rebuttal in their minds. This may work in the courtroom, but it does not go over well at home, with one's spouse or children, in particular with teenage offspring.

When practicing absorptive listening, even people who are not lawyers may notice the presence of an inner attorney—a mental voice saying, "Hurry up and finish talking so I can tell you what I think"—which interferes with tranquil, attentive listening.

People also discover how many times, even in a single minute, they "check out" while someone else is talking. There's a flick of the mind to a shopping list or a future appointment, or a flick of the eyes to notice someone passing by. Absorptive listening is not easy. It is a skill that takes time to learn.


DEEPER LESSONS

To do absorptive listening, we have to make the body and mind still. This is mindfulness in action, holding a core of stillness within, in a moving, noisy world. When you are listening carefully, you will be aware of your own thoughts as part of the landscape of sound. Like the sound of a passing car, you acknowledge your passing thoughts but are not disturbed by them.

If you are trying this practice with the support of a group or community, one of the most interesting aspects of this exercise is to be on the receiving end—noticing how you feel or react when someone is absorptively listening to *you*. Most people feel gratitude for being so well witnessed. They feel cherished.

There is a scene that has always touched me in the movie *Shall We Dance?* A man whose marriage has ended asks, "Why do people get married?" His companion says, "Because we need a witness to our lives. You're saying, 'Your life will not go unnoticed because I will witness it.'"

There is a Buddhist recitation for invoking compassion, and it highlights the role of listening in caring for others. "We shall practice listening so attentively that we are able to hear what the other is saying—and also what is left unsaid. We know that by listening deeply we already alleviate a great deal of pain and suffering in the other."

Therapists trained in absorptive listening say that it can, by itself, catalyze healing. There are types of therapy in which the therapist does not say anything, letting the wisdom emerge from clients as they listen to themselves talk.

One student who had been raised in a home where no one ever listened to him said that having someone listen to him with full attention felt like receiving "life-giving manna." Some people find it uncomfortable at first, as it is outside of their life experience to have someone *just* listen to what they are saying. They feel at first as if they are under scrutiny, like a biological specimen.

Absorptive listening can also give you equanimity with the difficult voices in your own mind. When the Inner Critic says something absurd like, "Look at your wrinkles. I hate them!

You shouldn't get old!" you can just be aware of what it says, neither believing it nor reacting.

---

Final Words: Absorptive listening is by itself therapeutic, and you don't need a degree in psychology to practice it.

---

## 39

# Appreciation

---

The Exercise: Stop throughout the day and consciously identify what you are able to appreciate in this moment. It could be something about yourself, another person, your environment, or what your body is doing or sensing. This is an investigation. Be curious, asking yourself "Is there anything I can appreciate right now?"

---

REMINDING YOURSELF

Post in appropriate places the word "Appreciate."

DISCOVERIES

Many people have tried using affirmations to make themselves happier or more positive in outlook, repeating phrases to themselves such as, "I am worthy of love," or "Today will be a good day and bring me what I want." Affirmations may be valuable at certain times, but they can also paper over a troubled mind-state. This mindfulness exercise is different.

Appreciation practice is an investigation. Can we find anything, anywhere, in this moment, that is cause for appreciation? We look, listen, feel. Anything? When we take a little time, we may find that there are many things to appreciate, from being dry, clothed, and well fed, to encountering a kind store clerk or the warmth of a cup of tea or coffee in our hand.

One category of things to appreciate is that which we experience as positive, such as having food in our belly. Another category of things to appreciate is the things that are absent, such as illness or war. We don't appreciate their absence until we've suffered their presence. When we recover from a bad flu, for a short while we are glad to be healthy again, grateful not to be vomiting or coughing, happy just to be able to eat and to walk. We don't appreciate health until we've been ill, water until we're thirsty, or electricity until it goes off.

This practice helps us stop, open our senses, and become receptive to what is available in our lives just now.


DEEPER LESSONS

This practice helps us cultivate joy. The Buddhist term for joy is *mudita*. It means more than just appreciating what makes us feel good. It includes the happiness we feel in connection with other people's joy and good fortune. This quality of joy is not hard to feel when the other people are those we love. For example, we can easily share our child's happiness with a new toy. What happens, however, when someone we dislike or are jealous of is given something we want for ourselves, such as public acclaim or an award? Can we feel joy in their joy? This is not so easy.

Have you ever noticed how the mind focuses on what is wrong—wrong with us, with people around us, with our work, and with the world? Our mind is like a lawyer reading the contract for "my life," always looking for flaws or contract violations. The mind is magnetically drawn to the negative. Just look at the news. What holds readers' or viewers' attention is natural or man-made disasters, wars, fires, shootings, bombings, recall of potentially dangerous toys or cars, epidemics, and scandal. Why is our mind attracted to the negative? It's because the mind doesn't have to be worried about the positive things that might happen. If good things come to pass, well, that's wonderful, but the mind quickly puts these aside. The mind's concern is protecting us from the negative, the dangerous.

Unfortunately, this means that negativity begins to color our awareness, often without our even knowing it. If we aren't aware of this subtle downbeat bent of our mind, it can grow unnoticed, leading to dark states of mind such as fear and depression. To counteract this tendency, to turn away from the mental habit of subtle negativity, to become more content with the life we are living, we need the antidote of mudita.

---

**Final Words:** Maezumi Roshi always admonished us, "Appreciate your life!" (He meant both our everyday life and our One Great Life. They are not separate.)

---

## 40

# Signs of Aging

---

The Exercise: This week, bring your attention to signs of aging in yourself, in other people, in animals and plants, and even in inanimate objects. How do we know something is aging?

---

REMINDING YOURSELF

Post the word "Aging" or pictures of an old person in relevant places, particularly on the bathroom mirror.

DISCOVERIES

This exercise generates a lot of insights and lively discussion at our monastery. When we pay attention, we see signs of aging everywhere. Fruit rots, flower petals wither and fall, buildings sag, cars rust. After about age thirty, young people report being dismayed that their body does not perform as well or heal as fast as it did when they were younger. I remember twisting my ankle and still feeling twinges and instability there a month later. I was indignant. Why wasn't my body doing what my mind wanted it to do, as it always had before? I still expected pain to disappear overnight, as it had in my teens.

A thirty-year-old reported that he didn't like being called a "man." His mind said, "No, my father's a man, not me." He didn't like noticing a few gray hairs. Many young people admitted resistance to "growing up" and assuming any degree of responsibility for this complex, fast-moving world. The choices seem bewilderingly endless, and the possibility of actually making a positive difference seems slim.

At about age forty, people realize that their life is at least half over. They might take stock and ask, "What unfinished tasks do I want to accomplish while I still have power in this mind and body? What dreams do I want to throw overboard?" After about age fifty, many people report that they look in the mirror and are surprised to see their parent or even grandparent staring back at them. How did I get so old? They are startled to look down and see wrinkles on their hands. (They appeared while I wasn't looking!) Or they are dismayed when they can't open a stuck jar lid or they "hit the wall" (of fatigue) hours earlier in the evening.

One woman in her seventies said she avoided looking in the mirror because she only noticed her wrinkles, which she hated. We asked the group, "How many people notice Betty's wrinkles when they talk to her?" No one raised their hand. Betty was surprised to find that no one but her own Inner Critic was upset about her wrinkles. Then one person said, "Well, I notice them because I think they're beautiful."

Dismay arises when our inner age does not match our body's age. One person speculated that our inner age gets stuck at the age in life when we were happiest. One man said, "I thought that when you got older, you naturally got wiser, but now I think you have to work at it." How to do this? he was asked. "I think you have to really start paying attention."

## DEEPER LESSONS

The essence of this exercise is to become aware of impermanence. All things are continuously aging and falling apart. We have to increasingly exert effort to keep them pulled together. I was once a guest in an immaculate and beautiful house. The elderly hosts had enough money to maintain it in every perfect detail. However, in the basement bathroom, which old age had made them incapable of visiting, I noticed a spot on the toilet seat where the paint was chipped. I had a sudden fast-forward image of this lovely house, left alone for a few decades, decaying and falling into ruin.

One person who did this exercise said, "I tried to become aware of all the things that are aging—this tea, this cookie, this carpet—but as my awareness widened out to everything, it became frightening and my mind closed down." Exactly.

One man tried to discover the precise sensation that told him how old he was. Was it a touch, a temperature, a sound, a taste? He could not find it. The notion of aging depends upon comparison. When you do not compare, there is only sensation, with no added attribute of age. My sense of smell is not as acute as it once was. I only know this, and can only suffer because of it, if my mind recalls a memory of a time when I could smell "better" and then mourns the loss.

We are better able to appreciate the changing phases of life-forms other than our own. We enjoy holding a tiny tomato seed in our hand. We grow excited when we see the first green sprout, and then we savor the red juicy fruit it produces. When the leaves and stalks of our tomato plant become brown and dry, we don't feel betrayed. We even relish the process of pulling up the dead stalks and adding them to the compost pile. It is much harder to enjoy each moment of our own life in this fresh, open way—baby, youth, adult, elderly, dying—with no before, no after, only this moment, just as it is.

---

**Final Words:** Resting in this moment, we have no age.

---

## 41

# Be on Time

---

The Exercise: For one week, work at being on time for all events. Consider what "being on time" means to you and to others. Watch what prevents you from being on time, and what arises in the mind when you or other people are late. (If you are a person who is always on time, you might try being a few minutes late and see what happens, externally and internally.)

---

REMINDING YOURSELF

Post pictures of a clock or watch in strategic places. Set your alarm five minutes earlier than usual for waking up and for appointments, to help remind you to be on time.

DISCOVERIES

Some people make it a habit to arrive early. They feel it is polite and part of being in harmony with a group. They may find themselves growing irritated with people who arrive late. Other people admit to being habitually late. They do not like having to wait for an event to begin—they feel bored or resent the waste of their time. Arriving early causes some people anxiety. They feel awkward when they are the first person to arrive at a meeting or dinner party. One person overcame that anxiety by using the extra time to help out or to relax and talk informally with the hosts or others who arrived early.

Some people scoot in "just under the wire." If one person arrives late to a recurring event such as choir rehearsal or a class, it seems to snowball, and others begin arriving late, too. This exercise brings up cultural differences. Trains in Japan and Germany are extremely punctual, so people are able to be on time more predictably than in the United States, where people in single-passenger cars fret as they sit unmoving in frequent traffic jams. One young American described calling the principal at the school where he taught in Japan to say he would be a bit late. He expected the principal to thank him for calling, but instead he was told, "In Japan we think about other people." He was almost docked a full day of pay for being thirty minutes late. From that time forward, he has never been late.

Some people set their clocks ahead deliberately, to fool their mind and thus be on time. Others set a false deadline in order to generate enough anxiety to get a task done on time. Some people found they were late because they had difficulty stopping what they were doing, or allotting enough time to clean up. Often people found they were late when they tried to cram too many activities into too little time, such as too many errands or one last e-mail before jumping into the car. Then they could not find their keys, necessitating a dash back into the house, a frantic search, a triumphant find, and the realization that they were late, again. Being on time may mean changing not just one but several habits, such as laying out your clothes or making your lunch the night before.

This exercise may uncover several inner voices. The Inner Critic may arise, saying, "You are so stupid! Can't you even tell time? You're always late! I think the boss is getting ready to fire you. Then how are you going to pay the rent or buy food? You're hopeless!" Another inner voice that may appear is the Rationalizer. As soon as you realize that you are late, this voice begins creating and rehearsing excuses. "My alarm clock didn't go off." "I got an urgent call/e-mail just as I was leaving." "Traffic on the freeway was terrible!" The naked truth is this: "I'm late." The only other thing that's worth saying is, "It's my responsibility and I'm sorry." That's it.

Some people are never late, and they might try a different exercise. They could watch the mind of judgment about others who do arrive late. Or they could take on the task of deliberately arriving late and then see what arises within their body and mind!

DEEPER LESSONS

This exercise is not really about time. It is about mind-states and habitual patterns. In other words, it is about the constructed self. If we think rather highly of ourselves, we begin to think that our time is worth more than other people's time. We prefer to be the last to arrive because we have so many important things to do and don't want to "waste time just sitting around and chatting." Perhaps our identity is tied to being highly productive and we don't see talking with our coworkers as producing anything of worth.

Or we may have a personality that is shy. We feel very ill at ease entering a room, trying to decide where to sit, looking people in the eye, and initiating a conversation. We'd rather slip in a little late and lean on our predictable small role in the meeting agenda than arrive early and agonize over what to do in an unstructured social situation.

Travel abroad often brings the realization that time is a human construct, a convenience, a convention we created to make events and people coincide. In many non-Western cultures, time is more flexible. The length of a day is governed by the duration of sunlight or even moonlight. A day in winter is shorter, a full-moon night longer. There is no exact time to meet. A meeting will occur when the time is appropriate. The time is appropriate when everyone has arrived.

Some people notice their mind saying that there is never enough time, which makes them anxious or even angry. "If they would only give me more time!" We have to ask our mind, how much time would be enough? How much time would be too much? In long silent meditation retreats, time becomes elastic. An hour can whiz by when the mind is still and focused. A few minutes can seem like an hour, especially when part of our body is complaining.

When we are thinking, we are dividing our life into chunks called time. There is the time of our future, which approaches, then arrives, and instantly becomes the time of our past. The present moment seems minuscule and ungraspable. When we are not thinking and are simply aware, we are aligned with the flowing nature of changing existence. The present moment is all there is; time becomes irrelevant. When we live more in awareness than in thinking, time seems to adjust so that there is exactly enough time for each thing to be accomplished fully, and then to disappear.

**Final Words:** In the present moment there is always plenty of time.

## 42

# Procrastination

---

**The Exercise:** Become aware of procrastination, the act of putting off something that needs to be done. Be aware both of the desire to procrastinate and of what you do about it—that is, your method of delaying. Look more clearly at what leads to procrastination, and see what strategies work to modify or overcome it.

---

REMINDING YOURSELF

Place the word "Procrastination" in key locations where you know you are likely to put off chores, such as the bedroom (near a pile of dirty clothes), the kitchen (near a stack of unwashed dishes), or the bathroom (on the messy medicine cabinet). You can also put notes in places or on things you tend to go to in order to procrastinate. You might put a sign on the TV, your video games, or even on your computer.

DISCOVERIES

When we discussed this exercise, most people were able to identify some activity—a phone call, a report, a letter, an application, an important conversation—that they had been putting off. One woman announced that she was just beginning to write her annual end-of-the-year letter to friends and family in February. She felt obliged to write a little personal note on each copy of the letter, which she anticipated would take another month. While examining procrastination she realized that she was delaying because once the letters were mailed, she might find that they were not perfect. This is an example of how the Inner Critic gets us coming and going. If she does mail the letters and they are not perfect, the Inner Critic will beat her up. If she delays in an attempt to make them perfect, and thus mails the letters late, or never, the Inner Critic will still be upset. There is no winning in the land of the Inner Critic. Its only job is to criticize, and it does this job well.

One person was putting off writing application letters, and found his mind making up excuses such as, "If it weren't for this or that, I'd have time to do this," when in reality, he was wasting the time he did have available. Another person discovered that she procrastinated at every step, sitting down to type a letter, editing the letter, printing the letter, finding envelopes and then the proper address. She said, "I think I have an idea in my head that each step will be much harder or take longer than it ever does."

We discovered many opportunities in the day to procrastinate or be lazy: leaving one dirty dish in the sink for later or for someone else to wash, dropping clothing on the floor at night, leaving the bed unmade in the morning, not picking up a piece of trash that missed the garbage can, leaving the last two squares of toilet paper on the roll to avoid having to change it.

This practice involves adopting a new motto: "Do it now."

One man realized that he procrastinated all day long, beginning with delaying getting out of bed in the morning. Someone else said he was able to overcome that problem when he realized that procrastination just made things worse. The more he put off getting out of bed, the harder it became to get up, so he now gets up as soon as the alarm rings. He found that if he delayed getting on his bike to ride to the meditation center, he would end up delaying so long that he would then decide not to go at all for fear he'd be late.

His conclusion was, "The mind with all its considerations just gets in the way of being wholehearted."

### DEEPER LESSONS

The antidote to procrastination is to take full responsibility. This includes taking responsibility for everything, from our personal messes, including the physical messes of a dirty mug or an unmade bed, to our psychological messes, including misunderstandings and mistakes. At my teacher's monastery in Japan, if you break anything, even a small dish that is already chipped, you must report it and apologize. Everything in the monastery is everyone's responsibility.

We become so busy with the many activities of daily life that it is easy to put off the most essential human task. In some religions that vital task is described as becoming one with God or becoming like Christ. In Buddhism it is called becoming awakened. We have some understanding of how important our spiritual practice is, but somehow it gets pushed aside by the many other things we must do to stay fed, clothed, sheltered, raise children, and so on.

Some people procrastinate because they opt for what gives immediate pleasure and takes little effort, such as going to a movie instead of finishing a term paper. They ignore the unpleasant consequences that will inevitably occur in the future. Others procrastinate because of aversion. They feel tense and overwhelmed at the thought of beginning a task and do not realize that putting it off only leads to more anxiety. Many good projects never get started or are never finished because of fear of failure or criticism once the project manifests. Some people avoid doing a job by escaping into daydreams or into alcohol-induced forgetfulness.

Procrastination is by definition counterproductive. It often brings about the very thing we are trying to avoid, suffering. The essence of mindfulness practice is to stop running away. We stop, turn around, and walk straight toward what we have been trying to avoid. We put it at the top of our "to do" list and tackle it first thing in the morning, before procrastination-mind wakes up.

One evening I visited a woman who was dying in middle age, from cancer. She had been a respected scholar, translating ancient Chinese texts about Buddhism. Now she was a skeleton covered in skin, lying in a huge white bed. She had only a few days to live. After we talked and I was preparing to leave she said wistfully, "I always thought I'd get around to actually practicing meditation later. Now there is no later." Recalling her words often helps me to sort out what is important and not procrastinate.

**Final Words:** If you were given a week to live, what would be the most important thing for you to do or say? Don't put it off.

## 43

# Your Tongue

---

**The Exercise:** For one week, while eating or drinking, become aware of your tongue. When you notice your mind wandering during a meal, return it to awareness of your tongue. It helps to ask questions such as, "What is my tongue doing or feeling right now?" Become aware of the changing experiences of temperature, texture, flavor, and spiciness. Where does it sense various flavors most acutely? How is your tongue moving?

---

REMINDING YOURSELF

Post images of a tongue in places where you eat.


DISCOVERIES

If you have difficulty watching what your tongue does, it helps to curtail its movements on purpose, and then resume eating very slowly and see what happens. Is it possible for you to sip a drink, take in a bite of food, chew, or swallow without the help of your tongue? People find that if they stop their tongue from moving and try to chew, chewing becomes a useless up-and-down chomping movement of the teeth. The tongue is a busy little being. It is almost never at rest. It helps us a lot during meals, with chewing, swallowing, tasting, and cleaning up. It darts quickly in and out of our teeth, mixing, moving, and dividing up the food evenly on both sides. It acts like a small janitor, probing with its sensitive tip into the corners of the mouth for leftover little bits of food, checking to see if the teeth are clean.

The tongue detects flavors, including the basic tastes of sweet, salty, sour, and bitter. Recent research shows that the tongue also senses umami (protein or savory) flavor, calcium, fat, minty-cool, spicy-hot, and metallic tastes. The tongue is also responsible for swallowing. It's interesting to try to see how it decides when it's time to swallow. As we do this mindfulness task, we quickly discover that it would be very difficult to eat, drink, or even talk without our tongue. The ancient practice of cutting out a person's tongue was a very cruel punishment indeed.

## DEEPER LESSONS

Tongue practice is one of the best examples of the power of mindfulness. When we focus the quiet mind on anything, that one small thing will open up and reveal an entire universe, a universe that was always there but somehow hidden. In the case of the tongue, it literally was hidden right beneath our nose. Ordinarily we are unaware of our tongue as it carries out its many tasks. We only notice it when we bite or burn it.

People are often amazed when they begin to pay attention to their tongue. "It's like a little man living inside my mouth, always taking care of things in there."

The tongue operates better when we let it alone. This is a good example of how things often function better if we can get out of the way and not try to control them. We could not possibly direct our tongue to do its job: "Move part of that bite to the right side. Look out! Here come the teeth, get out of the way! Time to swallow—no, wait! Not when I'm breathing in!" We could not design a computer program sophisticated enough to do what the tongue does for us.

Our tongue has been caring for us since before we were born, twenty-four hours a day, and we barely notice it unless we hurt it. This is one of the many ways we are supported and cared for in our lives that we do not notice or appreciate. We are largely unconscious of the continual presence of the earth below, which supports our every step, or of the air above, which contains the right mixture of 21 percent oxygen, 78 percent nitrogen, and water vapor necessary to support our life. As surely as we can become aware of the hidden life of our tongue, we can also, through practice, become aware of the many blessings of our life.

---

**Final Words:** The tongue has its own wisdom. Like most things, it operates better when we don't try to control it.

---

## 44

# Impatience

---

The Exercise: Become aware of impatience as it arises during the day. Be aware of the signals in the body (tapping fingers) and the talk in the mind ("Hurry up!") that accompany impatience. Ask yourself, "Why am I in a rush? What do I want to rush ahead to get to?" See what answers arise.

---

### REMINDING YOURSELF

Post notes saying "Notice Impatience" in your environment, especially in places where you know impatience is likely to arise.

### DISCOVERIES

Impatience is a common experience in our modern world. We become impatient when traffic slows or stops, when someone is late for a meeting, whenever we have to wait and "do nothing." Body signals of impatience are different for each individual. They include rapid heart rate, tapping fingers, jiggling legs, tightness in the chest or stomach, jitteriness. While doing this exercise I discovered that I always lean forward when I'm driving, as if driving is a waste of time and I could get there faster by leaning forward.

Mind signals of impatience include agitation, carelessness, irritability, and certain types of internal phrases, sometimes spoken aloud, such as "I can't believe how long this is taking," "What's the holdup?" "You idiot, get moving!" and many, more colorful utterances.

It can be interesting to look at where or when you learned to be impatient. Were your parents not patient? Did you learn it at school, because the teacher was uninteresting, or because the lessons moved too quickly or slowly? People afflicted with impatience often have trouble waiting for someone to finish speaking, interrupting with a premature reply because they think that they know what the person will eventually say, but can't bear to wait for them to say it. (An antidote is the practice of absorptive listening, described in chapter 38.)

Impatience depends upon the mind moving ahead into the future and trying to force or will time to move faster. People find that when they learn to recognize the early signs of impatience and turn their awareness toward any aspect of the present moment—their breath, the touch of clothing on the skin, the sounds in the room—impatience disappears.

DEEPER LESSONS

Impatience is an aspect of aversion, one of the three poisons described in Buddhist thought (the other two are clinging and delusion). The notion of its being "poison" is fitting since these three can literally make us mentally and physically ill. The term *aversion* refers to our mistaken belief that if we could just get rid of something or someone, we would be happy. If I could quit this job, or find a more loving partner, if all criminals could be put in jail, if we could get rid of all terrorists or Democrats or immigrants, if we could get rid of impatient people, then the world would be a good place for us to live. Impatience is one of the milder forms of aversion.

When the mind voices impatience or the body betrays it, it can be helpful to ask the mind, "We're in a rush to get this over with so that we can do what?" Typically the mind says, "So we can get on to the next thing to do." You then repeat the question, "So we'd like to get this over with and move on to the next thing so that we can do what?" With each answer, keep asking, "Then what?" You come to see that the mind is in a rush to get to the end of this hour, this day, and by logical extension, to get to the end of the week, the end of the year . . . and . . . to the end of life? As we rush, we have to remind ourselves that ultimately we are rushing toward the end of life. Is that really what we want to do?

We also rush to get through tasks we consider boring or tedious, such as washing the dishes, so that we can get to the things we consider interesting or relaxing, such as buying something online or watching a video. When we learn to bring moment-to-moment mindfulness to all aspects of our life, then the activities we were in a hurry to finish become interesting. When the mind is not straining at the leash to pull us into the future, then these activities can also be relaxing.

Impatience is a form of anger, and underneath anger/aversion is always fear. If the fear can be named, you can begin to dissolve the anger. Question: What is the fear underlying impatience?

It is fear of there not being enough time. This is both an unrealistic and a realistic fear. It is realistic because we never know when our life will end, and there are many things we want to do and experience before we die. Fear of not enough time is also unrealistic because time is the creation of our own mind. When we are able to quiet our mind, enter pure awareness, and match the flow of events, time disappears. The tranquillity of the eternal opens, and we are at peace.

---

Final Words: Impatience steals our life away. When impatience arises, drop into the present moment, breathing, listening, and feeling sensations.

---

## 45

# Anxiety

---

The Exercise: Become aware of anxiety. Notice all the body sensations, emotions, and thoughts associated with anxiety. Racing heart? Racing thoughts? Notice when anxiety first makes its appearance in the day. Does it appear as you drink coffee, as you watch the news, or as you arrive at school or work? Several times a day, pause briefly to assess whether anxiety is present within you. You may also notice what makes anxiety worse, and what relieves it.

---

### REMINDING YOURSELF

You can post little signs asking, "Are You Anxious?" in your environment, or images of anxious faces. Each time you notice one, pause to assess signs and symptoms of anxiety.

### DISCOVERIES

People are often surprised to discover that anxiety is a more constant companion in their lives than they thought. Anxiety is so pervasive in modern culture that people often don't notice it until their mind becomes quieter and more attuned, through mindfulness practice, to changes in the body and in the mind. It may pop up when the alarm clock buzzes or with the first ring of the phone. Some people find that they wake up already anxious. One woman said, "Anxiety is on the bedpost, waiting to pounce as soon as I open my eyes. If I keep my eyes shut, I can put it off." Other people find that anxiety is waiting with the morning news, with their first cup of coffee, or latches on to them during their commute to work.

Each person has different sensations in the body that signal "anxiety is arising in me." The heart may speed up, breathing becomes more shallow, the stomach tenses up, armpits tingle, then a leg starts to jiggle. Each person has different thoughts that accompany anxiety. "I'm failing, again." "He's going to leave me." "This is a hopeless situation." "I'm getting sick, and I'm going to die from this."

People who are able to recognize and then observe episodes of anxiety within themselves begin to see patterns, certain types of events or situations that are the seed from which anxiety quickly grows. Often these seeds were planted in childhood. One man whose brother choked him almost to death in childhood play became aware of anxiety arising whenever he wears tight collars or turtleneck sweaters.


DEEPER LESSONS

Anxiety is a manifestation of what the Buddha called "personality view," the notion that I am a separate and lonely self that is threatened on all sides by the "other." It is very important to learn to recognize anxiety in its earliest manifestations, and to develop tools to dispel it. Deep breathing is a powerful antidote.

We need to look to the bottom of anxiety in order to see through it clearly. Anxiety is always accompanied by thoughts, though these thoughts may be a form of inner talk that is too subtle to detect at first. Thoughts always refer to the past or the future, even the past a split second ago or a future a split second from now. When the mind rests in the present, we are not thinking. We are just experiencing. Even when the event is dangerous, such as a car accident, we are just experiencing it as it occurs, often vividly and in slow motion. The fear and anxiety come later. "I hit a patch of ice and skidded. I could have been killed. My kids would have been orphans! What if it happens again?" Thoughts can both give rise to anxiety and also escalate it. When we are driving and thinking anxious thoughts, we are not "just driving." We know that talking on the telephone while driving is not safe. What about talking on the inner telephone?

For most of our lives, we exist in one of two states: either upright, alert, and anxious (when we're awake); or horizontal, relaxed, and at ease (when we're sleeping). In meditation we are combining the best of these two states of being, moving toward a state in which the mind is calm but alert, the body is upright but relaxed, and the heart is open but strong.

As we see anxiety creep in, we become aware—"Oh, anxiety is present." Because sustaining anxiety depends upon thoughts, we turn the mind away from thoughts and toward a counteracting and wholesome practice such as deep breathing or loving-kindness. Gradually we learn to detect and disarm our anxiety earlier. The habit patterns or "mind ruts" it has created become weakened, and anxiety no longer has a hold on us.

Some people say, "Well, if I let go of anxiety, I'll stop making plans for the future. The very thought of letting go of anxiety makes me anxious. I'll turn into a jellyfish, just floating around, pushed by life's currents." They are confusing letting go of anxiety with letting go of planning. Anxiety and planning are different things entirely. Anxiety is the suffering that our mind layers on top of planning. Anxiety actually interferes with good planning. Anxiety is self-centered and it makes us lose objectivity. Good plans arise from objectivity, not emotion.

Here is an important clue about how to unwind the clutching fingers of anxiety from our heart. Find a way to switch from thinking to experiencing. In particular, switch to experiencing with the body, feeling the flow of breath, listening to sounds, obvious and subtle, looking at colors and patterns of light and dark. When we are truly present, time seems to slow and everything becomes more vivid. One thing follows another in perfect order, our worries drop away. All is well again.

---

Final Words: Anxiety is the subtle and pervasive destroyer of our happiness. It depends upon thoughts of past and future. It cannot exist in the present.

---

# 46

# Mindful Driving

**The Exercise:** Bring mindful attention to driving. Notice all the body movements, car movements, sounds, habit patterns, and thoughts involved in driving. (If you do not drive a car, you can bring attention to riding a bike or being a passenger in a car, bus, or train.)

REMINDING YOURSELF

Place a note on your steering wheel or dashboard. It's best to remove the note before you start driving, so as not to create a visual distraction, and to replace the note before you get out of the car so that it will be there to remind you next time you drive.

DISCOVERIES

People find that this exercise opens up beginner's mind, helping them to step back from driving on autopilot and supporting them in noticing all the subtle movements of driving. We can start this mindfulness exercise right after we get into the car. Feel the pressure of the seat on your thighs, buttocks, and back. Feel your feet resting on the floor. Feel the pressure of the metal key as you turn the ignition on. Feel the vibrations that tell you that the car is running and hasn't stalled. Notice how the hands grip the steering wheel. Top, sides, bottom rim? One hand or two? What emotions arise while driving? For example, people commonly report that when they are cut off by other drivers, they experience bursts of anger that destroy their mental serenity.

I like to pay attention to the feeling of the road, extending my awareness down through the tires into the pavement, as if the car body is my body and the tires are my feet. I pay attention to the bumps and vibrations as the car moves from driveway to street, street to highway. I listen to the sounds of driving, the engine sound, the wind sounds, the tire sounds.

I once drove the Japanese Zen master Harada Roshi from Washington to Oregon. As we crossed the state line, he seemed half asleep, but he immediately remarked on the change in road texture and sound. I was impressed by his continuous level of awareness and vowed to further develop my own.

When we practice mindful driving, we notice that each person has an individual style of driving. Some people drive slowly and timidly, making their passengers impatient, while others accelerate through yellow lights and make their passengers sick on sharp turns. Some drivers look at scenery, eat, and make phone calls while driving, others keep their eyes locked on the road, ready for any contingency.

Mindful driving calls for relaxed, alert awareness. When practicing mindful driving, I envision moving forward in what we call in Zen "one straight line." This means that no matter how many curves there are, no matter how many times you have to come to a complete stop and start up again, no matter how many detours you have to negotiate, you remain aware of your destination and steady in your purpose.

## DEEPER LESSONS

Because modern people spend so much time in vehicles, this exercise helps answer the question "When can I find time to practice mindfulness?" Being mindful in a vehicle can provide many minutes of extra practice each day and help us to arrive at our destination feeling refreshed. Like all mindfulness practices, mindful driving includes body, mind, and heart.

The fundamental question underlying all of these mindfulness tasks is this: "Are you willing to change?" Mindful driving involves being willing to change our driving habits. Normally we are only willing to change when life isn't working for us, if we are suffering. For example, we might become willing to drive no faster than the speed limit once we get an expensive speeding ticket. Mindfulness practice asks us to change ourselves for a different reason—out of curiosity, because change could lead us to greater freedom and happiness.

I was in a car as a passenger once while a Zen student of mine drove, and I commented on his inattentive driving habits. He immediately asked me, "Please tell me what you see and how I can change." I did and he did. Now he is a very good driver. This is the mind of a true student—to take anything that comes along as an opportunity to change in a way that benefits others.

If you want to experience more peace and contentment, you must examine all aspects of your life, become aware of what kinds of habit patterns you have accumulated in those areas, and be willing to discard any that are unskillful. Many people hope that one day someone will come along, or something will suddenly happen, like a flash of lightning, and transform their life completely. You can waste your whole life looking for happiness to arrive from the outside. A quiet, basic contentment is our birthright; it is already inside of us. Mindfulness gives us a vehicle that can drive us straight to the place where it lives.

---

**Final Words:** True transformation is difficult. It begins with small changes, changes in how we breathe, eat, walk, and drive.

---

# 47

# Look Deeply into Food

**The Exercise:** When you eat, take a moment to look into the food or drink as if you could see backward, into its history. Use the power of imagination to see where it comes from and how many people might have been involved in bringing it to your plate. Think of the people who planted, weeded, and harvested the food, the truckers who transported it, the food packagers and plant workers, the grocers and checkout people, and the family members or other cooks who prepared the food. Thank those people before you take a sip or a bite.

REMINDING YOURSELF

Post signs reading "Look into Your Food" in locations where you usually eat, such as in the kitchen or on the dining room table.

At the monastery we say a chant before meals that contains this line: "We reflect on the effort that brought us this food and consider how it comes to us." As with anything that you repeat several times a day, chanting these words does not mean that at each meal we actually think about all the people involved in bringing our food to our bowls. We might be vaguely aware of the cook in the kitchen and grateful to him or her if the meal is tasty. Hence this practice.

We have the advantage of growing much of our food at our monastery. Working in the garden and greenhouses opens our mind to how much work goes into bringing the lettuce and carrots to our salad. We are grateful to our neighbor as we shovel manure from his barn into our truck, shovel it back out of the truck, and layer it onto our compost pile along with scraps from the kitchen and clippings from the mower. Anyone who has helped with our annual canning gains a new respect for applesauce after picking many barrels full of apples from neighbors' trees, then washing, cutting, cooking, pureeing, and canning hundreds of quarts of fruit. Even though we are closer than most modern people to the labor involved in being able to sit down at a table of food and eat, when we do this deep-looking practice, we find that we still take many foods for granted, particularly those in packages, such as flour, sugar, salt, cheese, oats, or milk.

We do this exercise frequently, as part of our mindful-eating practice. It helps us to look with the inner eye in order to see the scores of people whose life energy contributed to the food

LOOK DEEPLY INTO FOOD ‖ 195

on our plates: the cook, the checkout clerk, the shelf stockers, the delivery drivers, the people in the packaging plants, the farmers, and the migrant workers.

When my husband and I had young children, we spent a few minutes in silence before meals contemplating who brought us our food. We were living in a big city, where most children thought that all food, including the fresh produce, came from the supermarket, mysteriously manufactured there behind the scenes, possibly from plastic. Even many intelligent adults do not know where food comes from. When a guest cooking soup at the monastery asked for onions, I went outside and returned with two I had pulled from the garden. He was appalled. What were those strange things with dirt on them?

Once the BBC did an April Fool's Day spoof on TV, a lovely news short on the abundant spaghetti harvest in Switzerland. (You can view it by searching online video for "spaghetti harvest Switzerland BBC.") The film showed costumed women gaily picking long strands of pasta from trees, and happy patrons being served "fresh-picked spaghetti" in restaurants. Many people contacted the BBC to ask where they could buy a spaghetti tree for their own garden!

DEEPER LESSONS

When we look deeply into our food, we become aware of our complete dependence upon the life energy of countless beings. If you pause to contemplate a single raisin in your cereal bowl and count the number of people who were involved in bringing it to you, going back to the people who planted, pruned, and weeded the grapevine it grew on, it is at least dozens. If you go back much farther, to the origin of cultivated grapes in the Mediterranean, it is tens of thousands. If you add in the nonhuman beings—earthworms, soil bacteria, fungi, bees—it becomes millions of living beings whose life energy flows toward you, manifesting as the raisin in your bowl and ultimately as the life of your cells.

To experience this is to understand deep within your soul the true meaning of communion. Each time we eat or drink, we are coming into union with countless beings. Life dies, enters our body, and becomes life again. This happens over and over until we die, when we give all that energy back. Our body disperses and arises again as many new forms of life.

How can we repay that many beings? Not with money. If we paid each person who handled this raisin a dollar, raisins would be the food only of kings. Can we at least honor them with our grateful awareness, with a mindful moment's appreciation of their hard work before we begin eating?

Zen teacher Thich Nhat Hanh says,

A person who practices mindfulness can see things in a tangerine that others are unable to see. An aware person can see the tangerine tree, the tangerine blossoms in the spring, the sunlight and rain which nourished the tangerine. Looking deeply one can see the ten thousand things which have made the tangerine possible . . . and how all these things interact with each other.

---

Final Words: The life energy of many beings flows into us as we eat. How best to repay them? By being fully present as we eat.

---

# Light

---

The Exercise: Expand your awareness of light in all its
forms, bright and dim, direct and reflected.

---

### REMINDING YOURSELF

Post the word "Light" or a symbol of a shining light bulb in
appropriate places, including on or near light switches.

### DISCOVERIES

This exercise is a wonderful example of how mindfulness
helps us see what we have learned to ignore. In the modern
world we take light for granted; however before electricity was
harnessed for our common use in the last half of the twentieth
century, light was precious, even sacred. At our rural monastery, power outages are not uncommon during winter storms.
As we try to cook or read in the small pools of light cast by
candles and kerosene lanterns, we understand why the Buddha

included light among the basic gifts one should give freely, along with water, food, clothing, shelter, and transportation. When power is restored after an outage, we appreciate light anew for a few hours, but soon go back to taking it for granted.

After experiencing a blackout, another mindfulness group undertook a variation on this exercise—practicing grateful attention each time someone turned on a light switch. They traced the flow of electrons from the light bulb backward, through the house wires, the lines, the substation, the generating plant, ending with gratitude for the long-dead plants and animals whose bodies comprise coal, oil, and natural gas. Can you pause now to appreciate the miracle of electricity and light?

Light enables people to use the hours after nightfall for self-improvement, entertainment, reading, studying, and creating things such as music and art. Light has an effect on our emotions; bright fluorescence and flickering candlelight each evoke a different mood. Some people become depressed as daylight hours shorten in winter. Light seems to spark energy and creativity in humans. When the hours of sunlight are few in Alaskan winters, people hibernate. In the summers, when the sun never sets, they come alive, even getting a little manic, and require fewer hours of sleep. Light is therapeutic. It has proven as effective as medication in treating simple seasonal depression.

Some people report that they love to soak up the rays of sunlight and are aware as they do so that all life depends upon the energy of light flowing from the sun. Recently, however, some people notice an aversion to sunlight, after all the warnings about tanning booths and sunlight causing cancer. The resultant fear of sunlight has caused the resurgence of an old medical problem—vitamin D deficiency. Recently doctors have had to advise people to get at least fifteen minutes of direct sunlight a day, as the sun's light helps us produce vitamin D.

While doing this mindfulness exercise, some people became aware of their eyes as organs that gather light and bring it into their being, so they also felt a new appreciation for the gift of sight. One person noticed that the beauty of colors and jewels depends upon light. She became aware of this while driving: traffic lights glowed like multicolored opals, streams of headlights moving toward her on the highway looked like a string of diamonds, and the brake lights ahead like many glowing rubies.

### DEEPER LESSONS

When we bring attention to light, we find it everywhere, as sunlight and artificial light, bright and dim light, direct and reflected light, white and many-colored light. It shines through green leaves, turning them into jade. It moves slowly across the floor, revealing the movement of the earth. It fills the bowl of sky above us, even when hidden by clouds or the shadow of the earth.

While becoming aware of light, people also became more aware of shadows and darkness. Light is so inexpensive and universally available that we seldom explore the darkness. There is light in darkness, often in unexpected places. If you go out into the forest at night without a flashlight, you may see many kinds of subtle light. This opens the other senses as well—hearing, touch, and smell. You find that you can follow a path by "seeing" it with your feet.

Dark and light seem like opposites, but actually each contains the other and depends upon the other. In the modern world we seem to be afraid of darkness. We leave so many lights burning all night in our houses, on our streets, and in our offices that we cannot see the light of the stars. Light is often spoken of as "good," and darkness as "bad," but if there were no night, we could not rest our eyes and our bodies.

Try becoming aware of the "darkness" behind your eyelids. You'll find that it is not purely dark there at all, but is filled with dynamic patterns of light and color.

It is a very interesting corollary to this practice to put aside scientific knowledge about light and regard it as if it were radiating out of objects. There is a Zen saying to contemplate: "Everything has its own light." This contemplation can include looking for the physical light each person or object emits or noticing the particular light each person brings to the world.

Light seems to give hope. Jesus said, "I am the Light of the world. One who follows me will not be walking in the dark, but will have the Light which is life." The Buddha's teaching is said to have "brought light into darkness" so that people could see the truth for themselves. The Buddha also instructed his followers to "be a lamp unto yourself," meaning that they should use the light of the mind to discover the truth. In the Tibetan Buddhist tradition it is said that our basic consciousness, the awareness behind our thoughts and emotions, has three inherent qualities—it is boundless, clear, and luminous or bright. This fundamental bright clarity means that the trained mind can cut, like a laser beam, through confusion and reveal the essence of anything we turn it to.

---

**Final Words:** Everyone has their own light. What is yours? Can you bring it forth to help give life to the world?

---

# 49

# Your Stomach

---

**The Exercise:** Become aware of sensations coming from the area you call "the stomach." Check in with this area before and after meals. What can your stomach tell you about hunger and fullness?

---

REMINDING YOURSELF

Post the word "Stomach" or simple images of a stomach in various places, including where you eat.

DISCOVERIES

In our mindful-eating retreats, I ask people to become aware of signals coming from their stomach. We explore the question "How do I know I am hungry?" We also ask people to check in with their stomach before, halfway through, and at the end of a meal, to see how full or empty it is. Many people are surprised to realize that they have lost touch with their stomach.

They are aware of sensations in the abdomen only when they are extreme, when the stomach is growling and complaining about being empty, or when it is "stuffed" full and complaining about being uncomfortably stretched. When people undertake mindfulness of the stomach, checking in with their stomach before meals, they often discover that they are sitting down to eat a complete meal even when the signals from the stomach say that it is already full. They are eating just because the clock says noon or six P.M.

Researchers from Columbia University showed that overweight people have a much greater tendency to ignore the signals from their stomach and be influenced by external factors such as how attractively the food is presented or even what time they think it is. If a clock is manipulated to read noon when it is actually ten o'clock, they will eat a full lunch. Normal-weight people will not, because they are attuned to internal rather than external signals to tell them when they are hungry and when they are full.

People who chronically overeat or binge on food are overriding the "I'm full" signal from their stomach. If they do this long enough, the signal strength seems to fade, and they have to learn to "listen" to their stomach again. The people of Okinawa are among the world's longest-lived. They have a saying, hara no hachi bu, which means "eat until you are four-fifths full" (literally eight parts out of ten). The first four parts support your good health, but if you eat that last fifth, it will support your doctor. People who learn to check in with their stomach several times during a meal almost always find that they feel quite satisfied with less food than they are normally accustomed to eating.

Mindful eating teaches us to pay attention to the wisdom

of our individual body. Some people find that their stomach is quite relaxed in the early morning and that hunger signals do not arise until ten or eleven o'clock. They have been eating breakfast at seven A.M. for decades because as children they were told that they couldn't do well in school if they didn't have a hearty breakfast. To their surprise, they discover that if they put off eating the first meal of the day until hunger signals arise, their energy level remains good and their mind is clearer. They may also discover that their body is asking for vegetables or soup for that late "breakfast," not their usual sweetened cereal or pancakes with syrup. Other people discover that they are like hummingbirds. They need an early breakfast and feel best if they eat small amounts often. Each of us is unique.

### DEEPER LESSONS

One mindful-eating exercise involves eating just one small bit of food, such as a single raisin or strawberry, very slowly, with full attention. Many people who do this exercise are amazed, when they check in with their stomach afterward, to find that they feel completely full. They exclaim, "How can I feel full after eating only one raisin? I've never eaten only one raisin in my life! What have I been ignoring?"

There is one aspect of feeling full that is physical. But there is a much more important aspect, the experience of satisfaction, that does not depend on the volume of food we put into our stomachs. It depends upon how completely aware we are of what we are eating. When we are mindful of the colors, aroma, flavors, temperatures, and textures of what we are eating, our satisfaction with any kind or amount of food increases dramatically.

I met a woman two years after she attended a mindful-eating workshop and was surprised to see that she had lost forty unneeded pounds. I asked her what she had done, and she said, "I asked myself why I ate. I realized it was because I wanted to bring my body to a sense of peace. So I began eating every meal mindfully, checking in with my body frequently as I ate. As soon as my body felt at peace, I stopped eating." Mindful eating opens our awareness to the full experience, the full satisfaction of eating. Mindfulness applied to all our activities opens our awareness to the full satisfaction of living a human life.

Some people confuse anxiety with hunger, because many of the sensations of those two experiences are the same—a gnawing feeling in the belly, difficulty thinking, feeling shaky or light-headed. If they eat when anxious, their unease may increase, because they are eating against their body and against what they know to be healthy. When we apply mindfulness, we can separate what the stomach is telling us ("I'm still full and busy processing lunch"), from what the mind is telling us ("I'm anxious because we have to finish that report by five o'clock"), from what our heart is saying ("I'm feeling lonely because my sweetie is out of town for three days"). Only when we know which part of us is hungry can we nourish ourselves in a healthy way. The food we need might be a sandwich, but it might just as often be a phone call to someone we love.

---

**Final Words:** Listen to the wisdom of your stomach. It can help guide you to better health and greater satisfaction.

---

## 50

# Become Aware of Your Center

The Exercise: Become aware of your center of gravity. It is located in the center of the lower abdomen, about two inches below the navel, and midway between the front abdominal wall and the spine in back. In martial arts this center of gravity is called the *hara* (in Japanese) or *tan tien* (in Chinese).

Whenever your mind wanders, bring your attention back to your center of gravity. Try to initiate all physical actions from this spot in your body—whether you're reaching, walking, bending, and so on. You can even chop food in this way. Let each chop of the knife originate in the hara, flow down the arm into the hand, into the knife, and through the vegetable.

REMINDING YOURSELF

In appropriate places post the words "Center of Gravity" or pictures of a body with a red dot in the lower abdomen to represent the hara. You might wear something under your clothing on your lower belly that will create unusual sensations to remind you of the task, such as a soft sash or a Band-Aid.

## DISCOVERIES

Ordinarily we initiate actions from our head. Our mind commands our arms and hands to reach out and pick up something that we want to use or eat. Our body is somewhat passive, waiting for the puppeteer in our head to pull the strings and hoist us up into action. In Zen practice and in the martial arts students are instructed to move in a more dynamic and integrated way, by becoming aware of their center of gravity, or hara, and allowing each action to flow from that imaginary spot. When they get up from a chair, it is as if the hara gets up and the rest of the body just follows. When walking, it is as if the hara is moving steadily forward, and the legs are merely moving beneath it. We can also stand with focus on the hara, knees slightly bent and weight equally distributed between the two legs.

People who play sports often make use of their center of gravity. A tennis player waiting for a return volley and a football player running with the ball both crouch to keep their center low. Their speed, flexibility, and agility spring from that center. A golfer rotates his body around that center when taking a swing. Paddling a canoe or kayak takes much less effort if the thrust and pull come from the hara.

Doing this mindfulness exercise, people often notice that they have more stability, better balance, and more physical power. They also discover that resting in the hara affects the mind. It becomes quieter, more focused, and the field of awareness widens. We might be sitting in a meeting, caught up in a heated discussion, but when we drop awareness into our center, we notice more of what is going on in the entire room as well as all the people in it, the sound of a ticking clock, or someone's nervous cough.

If people practice mindfulness of the hara long enough, they often find that there is also a stabilizing effect on their emotions. When a difficult emotion such as anger arises, if they drop their awareness into their center of gravity, the emotion stops growing and soon begins to fade. When you rest in your hara, you are like one of those blow-up toys with weight at the bottom. You can be pushed sideways or knocked over, but you will always bounce back and right yourself.

### DEEPER LESSONS

If you ask someone to point to where in their body they "are," most people in our culture will point to their heads. In Asian countries people tend to point to their chest (heart) or to their belly. My first Zen teacher used to walk by people and say, "You're up in your head." He could see when someone was lost in the confusion of whirling thoughts, and was reminding them to drop their awareness into their hara. My second Zen teacher tells his students to imagine that they have a second "head" in their belly, and to listen, speak, and move from that lower center. You will find that the mindfulness practice of absorptive listening (chapter 38) is enhanced when you listen from your center of gravity.

The center of gravity is very important to Japanese people. They have many expressions related to it, such as *hara no hito*, which refers to a person of hara, a person who has courage, integrity, determination, strength of will, and good character.

Conversely, *hara ga nai* describes a person who has no courage and lacks determination. *Hara ga oki* means a person with a big hara, someone who is generous, compassionate, and broadminded. *Hara o suete* means to settle the hara, to become calm and steady.

Although the hara is not an organ in the body, it is an energetic center, one that can be strengthened with persistent, mindful attention until, over time, it becomes a physically palpable quality of strong presence. I have met Zen masters who have developed so much hara-strength that it feels as if there were a huge boulder sitting in the room with you.

As you do the mindfulness exercises in this book, you may notice that many of them are based upon moving your awareness out of your head and thoughts and into your body. Our thoughts can never be about the present moment, because the present moment is an instant of pure physical sensation. For example, say our eyes catch sight of streaks of brilliant color in the sky. As soon as we have a thought about it, we are a split second removed from the pure sensation. When we think, "Oh, what a lovely sunset. Remember the one I saw in Arizona last year?" we are no longer just experiencing color and light. The mind has moved away from the experience to name what we see—"a sunset"—and is generating thoughts, memories, and comparisons *about* the sunset.

The thoughts aren't nearly as pleasant as the original experience—the sudden glimpse of red and purple in the sky. In fact the thoughts about the sunset can be very annoying, because they separate us from the natural pleasure of just seeing vivid color. This essential gap, the feeling that we are wrapped in a kind of cotton wool, that we are not really experiencing anything directly, is at the source of much of our discontent in life.

It is also the reason people try to amp up the intensity of everything, from the saltiness of potato chips or the caffeine jolt of various drinks to the volume of the car stereo.

The gap between us and everything else cannot be closed by adding intensity to our lives. It is our incessant thoughts that create that gap. When we move our "center of operations" from our mind to our hara, something happens. Extraneous thoughts settle, awareness opens up, and the uncomfortable sense of a gap between us and everything else dissolves. Try it!

---

Final Words: Any time you feel off balance, drop your awareness into your center. It will stabilize your body, mind, and heart.

---

## 51

# Loving-Kindness for the Body

---

The Exercise: For one week, practice loving-kindness toward the body. Spend at least five or ten minutes a day with this practice. It could be during your meditation time. Sit down in a comfortable chair and breathe normally. On each in-breath, be aware of fresh oxygen and vital energy entering your body. On each out-breath, send this energy throughout your body along with these silent words: "May you be free from discomfort. May you be at ease. May you be healthy."

Eventually you can simplify this process by just saying "ease" with the out-breath. Any time during the day when your attention is drawn toward your body (when you see yourself in a mirror or when you feel discomfort), send loving-kindness to the body, even if only briefly.

---

REMINDING YOURSELF

Post the words "Loving-Kindness for the Body" in critical places, such as on your mirrors, on the bedside table, or on the ceiling above your bed. If you'd rather use an image, it could be an outline of a body with a big heart in the center.

DISCOVERIES

A lot of people feel resistant to doing this practice. They keep "forgetting" to do it. Eventually they discover that underneath the resistance lies aversion toward their body. For our entire lives we have all been fed images of perfect bodies, and of people whose youth, wealth, surgeons, or steroids allowed them to create those bodies—movie stars, trophy wives, bodybuilders, professional athletes. Our ordinary bodies cannot compare, and subtle resentment toward the body can accumulate in the mind. My belly is too fat, my breasts are the wrong size, my legs are too short, my hair or eyes are the wrong color.

This used to be a struggle primarily for women, but advertisements have infected men with this pervasive displeasure as well. One young man disclosed that he has always hated his chest hair. This was surprising, since many men bemoan their lack of "manly" chest hair. He said he had been teased badly in junior high school when his chest hair grew in early. Although aware that the other boys were actually jealous, he was left with painful and enduring embarrassment.

Other people discover that they would rather be "in their head," thinking thoughts they can control, than practicing mindfulness of the body with all its mysterious and even frightening sensations. What does that short, sudden pain in my head mean? Could I have a brain tumor? There is so much that happens to our body that we cannot control, including getting sick, growing old, and dying. We can come to feel threatened or even persecuted by our body. Why won't it behave as a perfect, maintenance-free, perpetual-motion machine?

### DEEPER LESSONS

Nothing can thrive under bombardment by negative energy—not children, pets, potted plants, nor our body. When our body's appearance does not meet the standards of our Inner Perfectionist or Inner Critic, we may begin to feel subtly frustrated or angry toward it. This can also happen when a body part is in trouble, with injury or disease. We begin to fear or resent our body. This is not a healthy environment for our body, and can even create disease.

Loving-kindness is a palpable force, a healing force. People often find that when they send it to their body, they feel better physically. Mental tension creates physical tension, which restricts blood flow and constricts muscles. As I age, my body objects to getting up early in the morning. When I do loving-kindness practice for my body at the start of morning meditation, it's like taking two aspirin. When I do loving-kindness for my body before falling asleep, I can relax more deeply. And when I do it for my body when it's tired or sick, it feels like a healing balm. Loving-kindness puts all parts of us—body, mind, and heart—at ease.

Often people are resistant to send loving-kindness to themselves. They feel it is selfish and that they should be doing it for others who are in worse shape. Loving-kindness for ourselves is not selfish. It is a prerequisite for extending it to others. If our own reservoir of loving-kindness is full, it will naturally spill over and flow to others.

**Final Words:** Do loving-kindness practice for your body at least once a day, every day. It's the best kind of alternative medicine.

## 52

# Smile

---

The Exercise: For one week, please allow yourself to smile. Notice the expression on your face. Notice it from the inside—lips turned up or down? Teeth clenched? Tension and frown lines between the eyebrows? When you pass a mirror or reflective window, sneak a look at your expression. When you notice a neutral or negative expression, smile. This does not have to be a wide smile; it can be a small smile, like the smile of the Mona Lisa.

---

REMINDING YOURSELF

Post the word *smile* or a picture of smiling lips in various places, including on mirrors, and perhaps on your computer, on the dashboard of your car, on the back of the front door, and on your phone. You can try smiling when you talk on the phone, at stop lights, or whenever your computer shows the wait icon. When you meditate, try a soft "inner smile" like the smile on the face of the Buddha.

Some people feel resistant to doing this exercise. They feel that it is "fake" or unnatural to smile all the time. If they check a mirror several times a day, however, they may be quite surprised to find that all the time they were assuming that their face held a pleasant look, their habitual expression was actually negative—a slight frown, a downturn to the corners of the mouth that looks disapproving. Once people realize this, they often undertake to adjust their face to look more positive.

At the monastery we once tried a more extreme version of smiling practice called "laughing yoga." No matter how we felt, at nine A.M. we all gathered in a circle, rang a bell, and laughed for two full minutes. Laughter that seemed "fake" at first became genuine as we watched each other laugh. People found that once they overcame their resistance to smiling or laughing even when they didn't feel like it, these practices were quite enjoyable and induced a positive mood. Once a teacher assigned a somewhat morose student the practice of "grinning like an idiot" for an entire weeklong retreat. The man, a veteran of many long retreats, said it was the most relaxed, enjoyable one he'd ever done.

There is a lot of interesting research on smiling. In all human cultures, smiles express happiness. Smiling is innate, not learned. Every baby starts to smile around four months, even if they have been blind from birth. Babies show different smiles when they see their mothers ("genuine") and when approached by strangers ("social" smiles that involve the mouth but not the eyes). Smiles are powerful social signals. People shown pictures of different ethnic groups are more positively inclined toward any group shown smiling. Smiles help defuse anger in others; they can be distinguished from negative facial expressions at a hundred meters—the distance of a spear throw.

Research shows that smiling has many beneficial physiological effects. It lowers blood pressure, enhances the immune system, and releases natural painkillers (endorphins) and a natural antidepressant (serotonin). People who smile in a wholehearted way live, on average, seven years longer than those who do not have a habit of smiling. Smiling also makes people more likely to see you as more attractive, more successful, younger, and as someone they like.

## DEEPER LESSONS

Smiles are contagious. Often people who emerge from retreats are puzzled to find other people smiling at them, even strangers they encounter on the street or in a grocery store. Then they realize that their inner relaxed state has emerged as an outer smile, and that others are simply responding to that smile. The benefit is returned: when people smile back at us, our mood improves.

When we smile, it doesn't just affect the moods of others, it also affects our own emotions. There is feedback from the facial muscles to the brain. Zen teacher Thich Nhat Hanh says, "Sometimes your joy is the source of your smile, but sometimes your smile can be the source of your joy."

When you smile, and even when you simply stretch your mouth as if you were smiling, your emotions take an upturn. In fact, when people use Botox to erase facial wrinkles, their ability to move the facial muscles involved in smiling decreases, and so does the strength of their emotions, positive and negative. Research on smiling clearly shows that controlling the face can help control the mind and the emotions it produces. Dale Jorgensen, an expert on the effects of smiling, says,

> I've thought about this quite a bit. What I've found has reinforced one of my guiding principles, that we really are in charge of our destinies. We do have influence over what happens to us by virtue of our actions. Smiling is a case in which a simple act can have profound effects on the kinds of experiences we have with other people and how they treat us.

The Buddha is always depicted with a gentle smile on his face. It is an inspiring smile, a smile born of the joy of mindful awareness, of a person who is content in all circumstances, even at his death.

---

**Final Words:** If smiling has such clear positive effects upon us and those around us, perhaps we should take up a "serious" lifelong smiling practice.

---

## 53

# Leave Things Better Than You Found Them

---

The Exercise: This exercise carries the practice of "leave no trace" (chapter 2) one step farther. Try to look for ways, even small ways, to leave spaces or things cleaner or tidier than you found them.

---

REMINDING YOURSELF

Post the words "Better Than I Found It" in appropriate places, such as the kitchen, bathroom, or bedroom, and on the exit doors from these spaces.

DISCOVERIES

When people first try this exercise, they may become confused when they see how much *could* be done. Should I pick up all the trash on the sidewalk outside my apartment? How about in the street or the park? Where do I stop?

The best arena for this exercise is local and everyday, in the many little things we can all do, such as picking up a few bits of blown-around newspaper at the bus stop, wiping up the ring of spilled coffee on the kitchen counter, straightening the couch pillows as we walk through the living room, or using a paper towel to wipe out a sink in a public bathroom. Some young people said they found themselves hesitating to do this exercise because "then it might become expected of me." They said the expectations could come from others, such as parents, but also from themselves, as they began to feel guilty if they left things messy.

This task seemed to lend itself to what I call "mind poisoning." A few people got derailed by contemplating the philosophical implications of this task, wondering what "better" really meant in the scope of centuries of failed attempts to improve the world, or debating whether, if they found someone else's dirty dish in the sink, they should just wash it or whether that would "enable" the other person to continue being mindless and inconsiderate. However, as one person observed, "I discovered that if I didn't want to clean something, I was always centered on myself—'Why me? I don't want to do this!' If I thought about what would make other people happy, then the resentment disappeared and I found myself enjoying just doing the practice." Another person, on encountering a messy pile of other people's shoes, said that it was such a relief to drop her internal judgment and just engage the body in straightening them up.

People who relished this exercise experienced it as being linked to other exercises such as "saying yes" (to improving the state of things) and "secret virtue" (improving things without anyone noticing). One person extended the scope of this task from material things to people. She did this by asking "How can I leave this relationship better than it has been?" Another person tried a version he called "leaving the energy better." If he noticed that his state of mind was negative, crabby, or critical, he investigated ways he could change it to positive. In his case, singing was most effective.

### DEEPER LESSONS

There are endless ways we can work to make things better in the world. Although this exercise begins with improving our immediate physical environment, it has larger implications. Most of us are not going to invent something that will improve the lives of millions. (And, as we all now know, such inventions, from antibiotics to democracy to zoos, always have their dark side.) However, if every person worked with the goal of leaving their own small sphere of influence better as a result of their presence, the entire world would benefit tremendously.

In Zen practice we focus on improving the condition of the heart and mind. Many people noticed that when they found a mess that other people had made, they felt resentment about doing this exercise. They realized that their first task was to let go of resentment, and then they could dive into the task of cleaning, free of extra emotional suffering. As one person said, "I extended this task to include noticing and then cleaning up the clutter in my mind. I know that if I can let go of the judgment, criticism, and other unnecessary and unhelpful thoughts in my mind, I'm sure everyone I interact with, in fact, the whole world, will be better off."

Most people have a sincere desire to leave the world better off as a result of their passage through it. They use pollution-free cleaning products, take reusable bags to the grocery store, and are mindful of not wasting resources such as power, food, or water. These are ecological practices, ways of working to make the material world a cleaner, healthier place for ourselves and for generations to come. Spiritual practices are ways of working with our heart and mind, to transform difficult mental and emotional states such as anger, jealousy, and greed into beneficial states such as determination, joy in others' happiness, and generosity. The effects of these changes should not be underestimated. They radiate out to affect everyone we meet as well as everyone they meet, and they keep on spreading out from there, becoming another wonderful legacy we can leave for generations to come.

---

**Final Words:** It is not so hard to leave the world better as you pass through it. Just practice kindness.

---

# Beginning a Sitting Meditation Practice

Someone once asked me, "Do we need to learn to meditate? Isn't mindfulness enough?" It depends. Enough for what? Is mindfulness enough to make you happier? Yes. It is enough to dispel the common ennui, pervasive anxiety, subtle depression, and restlessness that often beset us. Medical studies show that mindfulness practice can relieve pain and many ailments of body and mind, from asthma to psoriasis, from eating disorders to depression. That simply being present, inhabiting our lives more fully, can make us happier and healthier is a truly wonderful discovery.

Mindfulness practices are a kind of meditation-in-action, or prayer-in-action. There is another aspect of mindfulness that involves sitting still. We often call it sitting practice. When the body is still, the mind can also become quieter. When the mind settles, we are able to get some space around the tangle of our thoughts. We have a chance to look deeply into the important questions of our life.

When the individual mind, with all its memories and worries, is still, we have access to a deep stream of wisdom that can emerge as insights, powerful enough to change the course of our life. That emergence is called by various names: openings, awakening to Truth, the voice of the divine.

No matter what it is called, when we are able to experience it within ourselves, our life is transformed. We are no longer afraid to live in this unpredictable, complex world. We know that we, like all beings, belong in this world, exactly where we are and exactly as we are.

Here are basic sitting meditation instructions. I encourage you to find a teacher who can guide you further.

### BASIC MEDITATION INSTRUCTIONS

Sit down on a chair or on a cushion on the floor. Sit in a way that feels relaxed but upright, allowing plenty of room in your chest and abdomen for breathing. (If you are unable to sit up, you can meditate lying down.)

Focus your attention on your breath. Find the places in your body where you are most aware of the sensations of breathing. Don't try to alter your breath; your body knows very well how to breathe; just turn your attention to the breath.

Rest your attention in the constantly changing sensations of breathing for the full duration of the in-breath and the full duration of the out-breath. Each time your mind wanders away from awareness of the breath (which it is likely to do often), gently bring it back.

This is the experience of being relaxed but fully present, as if we had awakened on a vacation day, with nothing special to do except to take simple pleasure in just sitting and breathing.

Continue for up to twenty or thirty minutes, a good amount

of time for one meditation session. It is also fine to go longer. It is best to meditate every day, making this part of your personal health care, like taking a shower (for your mind). On a very busy day you may have to cut the time. Five or ten minutes each day is better than two hours once a month. I find that each minute of meditation is returned twofold or more in clarity, equanimity, and efficiency during a busy day.

FURTHER WAYS TO PRACTICE

Some of the exercises in this book can be extended into periods of meditation, contemplation, or prayer. Be creative. Here are a few examples:

CHAPTER 4: APPRECIATE YOUR HANDS

As you meditate, open your awareness to the feelings within your hands, particularly where they touch each other. Christians may wish to meditate upon "These are the hands of God."

CHAPTER 16: JUST THREE BREATHS

During meditation, for three breaths, keep your mind completely open and receptive, free of thoughts. Then relax and let your mind wander as it will. In a few minutes, once again, let all thoughts drop and pay full attention to the subject of prayer or meditation for just three breaths. Repeat.

CHAPTER 23: EMPTY SPACE

Make space the focus of your meditation. For example, become aware of the space in your body (lungs), the space in the room, and the space in your mind—in between your thoughts.

### Chapter 38: Listen Like a Sponge

During meditation or contemplation, listen very carefully to all the sounds you hear, both obvious and subtle. Listen as if at any minute you might hear an important message.

### Chapter 48: Light

Meditate on the flame of a small candle placed three to six feet away, or meditate in complete darkness.

# Suggested Reading

The following are a few of the most clearly written and popular books on mindfulness:

Bhante Henepola Gunaratana, *Mindfulness in Plain English* (Boston: Wisdom Publications, 1991).

Thich Nhat Hanh, *The Miracle of Mindfulness* (Boston: Beacon Press, 1996).

Thich Nhat Hanh, *Happiness: Essential Mindfulness Practices* (Berkeley: Parallax Press, 2009).

Jon Kabat-Zinn, *Full Catastrophe Living: Using the Wisdom of Your Body and Mind to Face Stress, Pain, and Illness* (New York: Delacorte Press, 1990).

Jon Kabat-Zinn, *Wherever You Go, There You Are* (New York: Hyperion, 1994).

You may also be interested in reading my previous book, *Mindful Eating: A Guide to Rediscovering a Healthy and Joyful Relationship with Food* (Boston: Shambhala Publications, 2009).

# Acknowledgments

I am grateful to my teachers, Zen masters Maezumi Roshi and Shodo Harada Roshi. I have learned much about mindfulness by watching them do ordinary tasks such as opening envelopes or making tea. I am grateful to all the people who have undertaken these mindfulness exercises so earnestly over the past twenty years and who passed their discoveries and insights on to me. I am also grateful to Eden Steinberg, whose unfailing editorial eye helped create a better book than I could write alone.

# About the Author

JAN CHOZEN BAYS, MD, is a pediatrician, a meditation teacher, and the author of *Mindful Eating*. She is also the abbess of Great Vow Zen Monastery in Oregon, where the mindfulness exercises in this book were developed and refined. She is also a wife, mother, and grandmother. She likes to garden, work in clay, and play marimba. For more information visit www .greatvow.org/teachers.htm.